AQA Performing Arts

GCSE

Mike Allen
Annie Bainbridge-Ayling
Eddie Brierley
Helen Curson

Series editor
Annie Bainbridge-Ayling

Nelson Thornes

Text © Mike Allen, Annie Bainbridge-Ayling, Eddie Brierley and Helen Curson 2009

Original illustrations © Nelson Thornes Ltd 2009

The right of Mike Allen, Annie Bainbridge-Ayling, Eddie Brierley and Helen Curson to be identified as the authors of this work has been asserted by them in accordance with the Copyright, Designs and Patents Act 1988.

All rights reserved. No part of this publication may be reproduced or transmitted in any form or by any means, electronic or mechanical, including photocopy, recording or any information storage and retrieval system, without permission in writing from the publisher or under licence from the Copyright Licensing Agency Limited, of Saffron House, 6–10 Kirby Street, London, EC1N 8TS.

Any person who commits any unauthorised act in relation to this publication may be liable to criminal prosecution and civil claims for damages.

Published in 2009 by:
Nelson Thornes Ltd
Delta Place
27 Bath Road
CHELTENHAM
GL53 7TH
United Kingdom

09 10 11 12 13 / 10 9 8 7 6 5 4 3 2 1

A catalogue record for this book is available from the British Library

ISBN 978 1 4085 0422 2

Cover photograph/illustration by Alamy / Jupiter Images/ Brand X

Illustrations by Pantek Arts Ltd

Page make-up by Pantek Arts Ltd, Maidstone

Printed and bound in Spain by GraphyCems

Photo Acknowledgements
Getty Images; 5.1F, 8.0A, AFP Intro Aii, 7.0A, PM Images 5.6Mi: Alamy Images; Jupiter Images/Comstock images Intro Ai, Jupiter Images/BananaStock 5.7N, Paul Wood Intro C, Keith Morris Intro E, 1.3I, Mike Goldwater Intro Fiv, Robert Harding Picture Library 1.0B, Adrian Sherratt 1.7O, Chris Lobina 5.1E, Photos 12 5.1Giv, Paul Springett 05 7.0B, Andrew Woodley 7.0D, Paul Gapper 7.1F, Mira 7.1H, Diana Bier Venice Carnival 7.6J, Pete M. Wilson 7.7K, Jim West Unit 4 opener: Fotolia; Earl Robbins Intro Aiii, Pavel Sazonov 1.1E, Thomas Owen 7.1E: Rex; 2.4H, 2.4I, 5.1G, 5.3J, 6.0A, 6.1E, 7.1G: Corbis; The Gallery Collection Unit one opener, Gero Breloer /EPA 1.0C, Peer Grimm/EPA 1.1D, Ruben Sprich/Reuters 1.1F, Patrick B Kraemer/EPA 1.2H, Nicolas Six / Danser 5.0C, Cultura 5.6Mii, Simela Pantzartzi/epa 6.0C, Robbie Jack 6.0D, Stephane Cardinale/People Avenue 6.1F, Bettmann 6.1G, 6.2I, Jacques M. Chenet 6.3L, Matthieu Colin/Hemis 7.2I: Lebrecht Music & Arts; Jason Temple 6.2H, Tristram Kenton 3.6E: Photolibrary; Karl Johaentges 1.4M, BananaStock 1.3J, 1.4L, 5.5L, Digital Vision 2.5J, Comstock 3.2B, Nordic Photos 5.4K: iStockphoto; Intro Fiii: Reproduced by kind permission of Katie Henry, Orange Tree Theatre; Intro Fii, 1.4K, 4.0B, 5.1D, 5.3H, 6.2K: Reproduced by kind permission of Kings Theatre, Southsea 1.6N, 5.6Miii: Reproduced by kind permission of Everyman Theatre, Cheltenham 2.0A, 2.1C, 2.1E: Reproduced by kind permission of Clwyd Theatr Cymru 2.3G: With thanks to Bishop's College, Gloucester 4.0A: Reproduced by kind permission of the National Theatre 3.4D: Reproduced by kind permission of M6 Theatre 3.0A: From the Education Resource Pack, written by Helen Cadbury, for Pilot Theatre's production of Looking For JJ 1.2G: Michael Le Poer Trench © Cameron Mackintosh Ltd 6.2J: Helen Curson; Intro D: Courtesy of David Faulkner; 5.3I.

Text permissions
Page 31 Excerpt (9 words) from page 716 from "Oxford Companion to the Theatre" by Hartnoll P (1967).

Contents

Introduction — 5

UNIT ONE: Skills development

1. The Olympics past and present — 16
2. Pantomime — 31
3. Every child matters — 39

UNIT TWO

4. Final showcase performance — 46

UNIT THREE: Working to a commission

5. Street life — 52
6. Musical theatre — 68
7. Carnival! — 76

UNIT FOUR

8. Final performance/designs for the chosen commission — 86

Glossary — 90
Index — 92

Nelson Thornes and AQA

Nelson Thornes has worked in partnership with AQA to make sure that this book offers you the best possible support for your GCSE course. All the content has been approved by the senior examining team at AQA, so you can be sure that it gives you just what you need when you are preparing for your exams.

How to use this book

This book covers everything you need for your course.

Learning Objectives

At the beginning of each section or topic you'll find a list of Learning Objectives based on the requirements of the specification, so you can make sure you are covering everything you need to know for the exam.

Objectives
Objectives
Objectives
Objectives
First objective.
Second objective.

AQA Examiner's Tips

Don't forget to look at the AQA Examiner's Tips throughout the book to help you with your study and prepare for your exam.

AQA Examiner's tip

Don't forget to look at the AQA Examiner's Tips throughout the book to help you with your study and prepare for your exam.

AQA Examination-style Questions

These offer opportunities to practise doing questions in the style that you can expect in your exam so that you can be fully prepared on the day.

AQA examination questions are reproduced by permission of the Assessment and Qualifications Alliance.

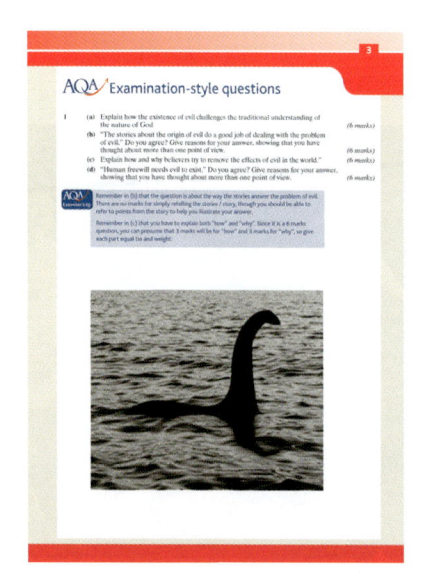

Visit www.nelsonthornes.com/aqagcse for more information.

AQA GCSE Performing Arts

Objectives

In this section you will learn:

what the performing arts involve

that the performing arts are a practical subject

what you will do in the course.

Did you ever stop to think about the impact that the performing arts industry has on our lives? Television programmes, films, musicals, theatre, carnivals, rock and pop concerts are just a few examples of how the performing arts entertain us and provide us with ways of understanding and sharing different cultures. Listen to conversations around you and you will often hear discussions of what has been happening in the 'soaps' or the latest 'reality show'. People talk about films and there is often strong demand for merchandise based on the heroes and heroines. Compact discs of favourite singers or groups and DVDs of their performances are prized possessions.

A *Different types of performances*

In GCSE Performing Arts you are about to start on a journey that will introduce you to this exciting and challenging world. You might have been involved already in some aspects of the performing arts either as a performer or as a member of an audience. You might have experienced some of the skills you will need to succeed – but you may also meet some that are new to you. The important thing is that you enjoy the experience and build your skills and confidence as you work through the course.

This book will help you to work through the **practice briefs** and **commissions**. The advice and information given are also important and should underpin your work.

> **Key terms**
>
> **Practice brief**: example of the kind of pieces set by the awarding body for practical assessment in Unit 2 and forming the basis of the portfolio evidence that you collect in Unit 1.
>
> **Practice commission**: example of the kind of work that you will include in your portfolio for Unit 3, which gives you opportunities to prepare for the commission set for Unit 4.

Why choose Performing Arts?

The performing arts are not just about creating performances; they also affect our leisure activities. If you have been to Disneyland or other theme parks where performers entertain the crowds, or on a cruise with different performances every night, you will understand how performing arts can be used to enhance the experience of the customer.

When people watch a TV programme, parade or concert in performance, they see the performers. It is certainly true that the actors, dancers, DJs and musicians who are in front of the audiences getting the applause are important and it is this aspect of the performing arts that may have attracted you to the subject at first. However, the audience do not see the workers in the industry who support those performers.

Working with other people

A vast array of technicians, artists, and designers work behind the scenes, preparing lighting, sound, sets and costumes before the performance and then supporting the performers during the show.

The performance would not happen without these people working in the background. There would be no microphones, lighting laser displays, special effects, costumes or musical backing. Cues would be missed because there would be no stage manager to coordinate them. There would be no audience because there would be no publicity and tickets would not have been sold. All the different roles and responsibilities must work in partnership with each other if the performance is going to happen.

Learning new skills

The most exciting and challenging aspects of the Performing Arts course is learning how this partnership works. You will take an active part in planning and creating performances. By working as part of a group you will learn how performances are put together from the initial ideas, through planning and rehearsals, to the final performance in front of an audience.

What will I be doing on this course?

The first thing that you will realise about GCSE Performing Arts is that it is very much based on your practical involvement in workshops, rehearsals and research. You will be expected to develop a range of skills that are directly linked to the creation and performance of a **showcase** or commission for an audience.

The course will introduce you to 17 performance disciplines that are essential to an understanding of the demands of the performing arts. You will need to think carefully about the skill areas because they will determine the kind of performances you will create.

Diagram **B** shows the disciplines involved and you should take time to discuss it with other members of the group and your teacher. You will be familiar with some of the disciplines but some may be new to you. As you work through this course, you will be able to select those that you feel best show your potential as a performer. It is worth considering that other members of your group will have different disciplines to contribute and will therefore allow you to explore the themes and ideas in the practice briefs and commissions from a range of approaches. It is expected that you will have a fairly broad knowledge of more than one of the performance disciplines but you shouldn't feel pressured to cover them all.

You will work through a series of practice briefs and commissions and build evidence for your **portfolios** through research and recording of your practical work. You will be encouraged to experience the work of others by attending performances and reviewing their work. Throughout the course you will develop your skills by working as part of a group and possibly, at times, as an individual. You will need to be well organised and prepared to work hard if you are to achieve the very best results.

It is important that you start to think about the best way to develop your skills and record your progress. Your teacher will advise you about the best way to do this but it will be useful to follow the seven steps to success that are used in the practice briefs and commissions in Units 1 and 3.

When you organise your portfolio you will find it useful to keep the 'steps to success' in mind as you build the evidence for each section.

> **Key terms**
> **Showcase**: a performance that is created to show the skills of the group to best advantage; it has a theme and structure that suits the demands of the given brief.
> **Portfolio**: a record of the work that you have completed during the course.

Physical performance skills
Acting, dancing, singing, music (instruments)

Physical design and making skills
Costume, make-up, puppets, masks, set design, properties

Performance

Technical management skills
Music technology, DJ-ing, stage management, lighting, sound

Administration
Front of house, marketing and publicity

B *The performing arts disciplines*

How will my work be assessed?

The Performing Arts GCSE is offered as either a single GCSE (Unit 1 and Unit 2), or as a double award (Unit 1, Unit 2, Unit 3 and Unit 4). The course is very practical and relies on you working as an individual and as a key member of a group.

Your teacher will assess your work and it will be externally moderated. The assessment grid published in the specification provides a clear set of criteria to use when assessing your work. Your teacher will have copies of the assessment grid and should spend time explaining the different stages to you as you work through the course. You will need to refer to the assessment grid when writing your peer assessments and witness statements. If you have any doubts at all or questions about your work, remember your teacher is there to help.

The assessment process expects you to provide evidence of research, practical involvement in a range of workshops and activities including performances, and evaluations of your own and others' work. It is very important that you include a series of **skills audits** with each of your practice briefs and commissions.

Each unit has specific assessment criteria and should be referred to throughout the course. You will see that the criteria for Unit 1 (skills development) differ from the criteria for Unit 2 (showcase performance) and the criteria for Unit 3 (working to a commission) differ from the criteria for Unit 4 (final performance/design for the chosen commission). You will need to discuss the criteria with your teacher in order to understand what is involved so that you can develop your skills and performance work.

It is important to make sure that the work for each unit is clearly organised and evidence for all your work is well presented. If you intend to complete the double award you will need to complete all four units and have separate portfolios for Unit 1 and Unit 3.

> **Key terms**
>
> **Skills audit**: a detailed check or inspection of what skills you have as an individual and as a group.

C *A performance in progress*

How to build your portfolio

Building your portfolio is a very important part of the process that you are about to undertake. The portfolio for Unit 1 Single GCSE carries a total of 60 per cent of your final mark and therefore the work recorded in it should reflect its importance.

The portfolio should clearly show your involvement in and understanding of the performing arts. It is your opportunity to have ownership of the course and explore and research the different aspects of the work you undertake.

Your portfolio should have evidence of everything you have done. You can include:

- skills audit sheets
- minutes of meetings
- research materials
- evidence of job roles and an understanding of the work-related context of your work
- photographs of rehearsals, performances, models and completed designs
- planning sheets
- evaluations
- peer assessments and witness statements
- designs for lighting, costume, set, props and sound
- cue sheets and running orders
- information regarding the range of venues that you use for the performances
- original scripts
- notes and diary entries of rehearsals and workshops.

Take pride in the final portfolio and present it in a clear and organised way. It will help your teachers and the moderation team if you work to the following example.

Portfolio for Unit 1

Your portfolio for Unit 1 should include the following items:

- Front sheet clearly stating your name and candidate number. Your teacher will provide you with:
  - An official AQA candidate record form, which you must sign. The teacher must complete it by filling in the marks on the back.
  - A completed assessment grid, filled in to show your final mark.
- Contents page giving page numbers and headings for each section.
- Initial skills audit that shows your starting point and gives you a base from which to chart your progress. It will also tell your teacher what you can do, especially if you do performance work out of school. Photocopy any certificates and qualifications to put in this section or performance programmes and photographs of you performing.
- Information about workshops and other practical activities that show how you have gained your skills and how you have begun to develop them. Remember to reassess your skills audit.
- Observations and witness statements.

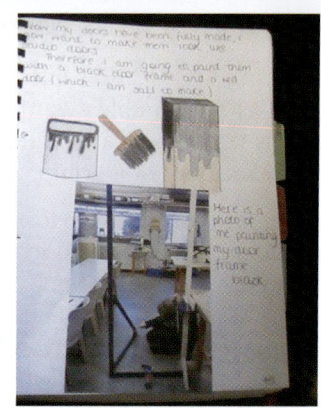

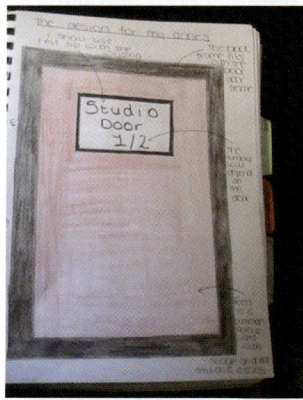

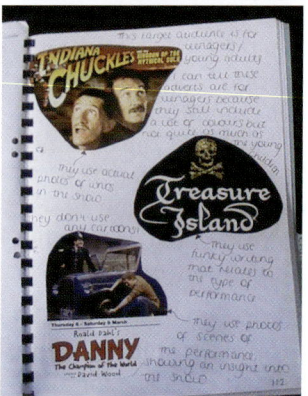

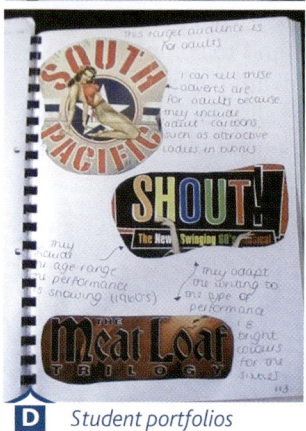

D *Student portfolios*

- Practice briefs:
  - These will each need a title page that gives the name of the brief – for example, 'the Olympics' – and dates when it was started and performed.
  - A record of all the materials that you have developed and used in the rehearsal and planning stages of a brief and details of the final performances.
  - You will then evaluate the process and update your skills audit ready for the next practice brief.
- The final showcase. This section will record all the work that you have undertaken in preparation for the final performance of your Showcase for Unit 2. It is vital to state how you will show your skills to the best advantage. It will also include the evaluation of your performance.

Portfolio for Unit 3

Your portfolio for Unit 3 double award carries a total of 30% of your final mark and should include the following items:

- Front sheet clearly stating your name and candidate number. Your teacher will provide you with:
  - an official AQA candidate record form, which you must sign and the teacher must complete by filling in the marks on the back
  - a completed assessment grid filled in to show your final mark.
- Contents page giving page numbers and headings for each section.
- Initial skills audit that shows your starting point and gives you a base to chart your progress. It will also tell your teacher what you can do, especially if you carry out performance work out of school. Photocopy any certificates and qualifications to put in this section or performance programmes and photographs of you performing.
- Information about workshops and other practical activities that show how you have gained your skills and begun to develop them. Remember to reassess your skills audit.
- Observations and witness statements.
- Practice commissions:
  - These will each need a title page that gives the name of the commission – for example, musical theatre – and dates when it was started and performed.
  - A record of all the materials that you have developed and used in the rehearsal and planning stages of a brief and details of the final performances.
  - You will then evaluate the process and update your skills audit ready for the next practice brief.
- Planning for the final performance/designs for the chosen commission planning. This section will include the proposals, plans, research and minutes of meetings that reflect the planning process.
- The final performance/designs for the chosen commission. This section will record all the work that you undertake in preparation for the final performance for Unit 4. It will also include the evaluation of your own and others work.

> **AQA Examiner's tip**
> - Take photographs of artefacts such as set models, costumes and other bulky items to put in the portfolio. Your teacher can provide an artefact sheet to record any bulky items that cannot be included in the portfolio and are kept in school.
> - Remove downloaded sheets that have not been annotated and unwanted materials.
> - Number the pages after you have edited the contents.

Evaluation

Evaluation of your work and that of others forms an important part of what you are about to undertake. You will need to keep notes of the work that you and the other group members do as they will be very useful when it comes to writing your final evaluations.

You will need to include details of:

- your own work
- planning and research
- knowledge and understanding of work-related aspects of the performing arts
- the work of other people, especially those in the industry.

You will find activities to help you complete the evaluation process in Practice showcase brief 1 (chapter 1).

Evaluation of your own work and that of other people is an essential part of the performing arts process. Evaluation allows you to update your skills audit and to plan the development of skills that need more work or to learn any new skills that are needed for your planned performances.

Roles and responsibilities

As you work through the course you will be able to develop and explore the different aspects of the performing-arts process. This will lead to you having to take on roles and responsibilities that are new to you. It will not be enough to focus on the performance skills of acting, dancing and singing, for example; you will also need to understand what is involved in working effectively as part of the front-of-house team or what is required to market and advertise your performances. You will be given the opportunity to carry out a wide range of roles and responsibilities in order to understand the different aspects of performing arts process. These will include stage management, design and technical support as this will help you to understand the demands of performance. No matter what your final roles and responsibilities are, you are still expected to work as part of a team.

> **Remember**
> You may take on more than one role and be responsible for a number of important aspects of the production process.

As you work through the practice briefs and commissions in this book you will have opportunities to take on these new roles and meet the demands and responsibilities set for each performance. You need to be aware of all aspects of the process and make sure that you include your observations in your evaluations.

E *Sound technician, one of many roles available to you*

How this book works

Each unit of this book corresponds to a unit of the course:

- Unit 1 contains practice briefs that you should complete and record in your portfolio for Unit 1, skills development.
- Unit 2 outlines the main points to be aware of as you work towards the practical examination for Unit 2, showcase performance.
- Unit 3 contains practice commissions that you should complete and record in your portfolio for Unit 3, working to a commission.
- Unit 4 outlines the main points to be aware of as you work towards the practical examination for Unit 4, final performance/designs for the chosen commission.

The research that you undertake while working through Units 1 and 3 provides you with the opportunity to develop all the skills areas set out in the specification. Your teacher will spend some time talking you through the process and will support you in developing your skills by providing practical workshops and rehearsal periods. This book sets out a series of activities to focus your work and suggests areas that you might find interesting to research. It is worth remembering that you may have ideas of your own and you should include these as well. The illustrations in each section can be useful stimuli for discussion and starting points for further research and possible design work.

The information given in Units 2 and 4 will help you to focus on the tasks set by AQA and to develop your understanding and skills.

All that remains is to wish you luck and hope that you enjoy working towards your GCSE in Performing Arts.

F *This is a multi-faceted subject*

UNIT ONE and UNIT TWO

GCSE Performing Arts is offered as a single GCSE and a double award. You must complete Units 1 and 2 for the single GCSE. For the double award, you must also complete Units 3 and 4, which are covered later in this book.

UNIT ONE   Skills development

Internally assessed and externally moderated.

Marked out of 70 (60% of the total marks for the single GCSE)

Students experience skills' development and professional conduct through practical involvement.

Practice showcase brief 1
The Olympics past and present

Practice showcase brief 2
Pantomime

Practice showcase brief 3
Every child matters

UNIT TWO   Showcase performance

Internally assessed and externally moderated.

Marked out of 60 (40% of the total marks for the single GCSE)

Students work as a production company to put on a performance in response to a showcase brief

Exam period 1 February – 31 May

Showcase performance

Key terms

Showcase performance: the programme of pieces that are rehearsed and shown in the final performance.

In Unit 1, you will develop your skills in the performing arts disciplines and will gather evidence of what you learn. What you do in this unit will provide you with the fundamental skills, knowledge and understanding which you will use in Unit 2.

Your portfolio of evidence will reflect the work you do, your personal skills and your understanding of planning and presenting a performance.

In Unit 2, the work you do is based on the work carried out in Unit 1. Unit 2 gives you the chance to demonstrate what you have learned about working as part of a team and how to present your personal skills. You work with the rest of your performing arts group to produce a showcase performance to meet a brief set by AQA. You should include the work you do for the showcase performance in the portfolio you compile for Unit 1.

In both Units 1 and 2, you will follow a process that includes the seven steps to success.

Seven Steps to Success

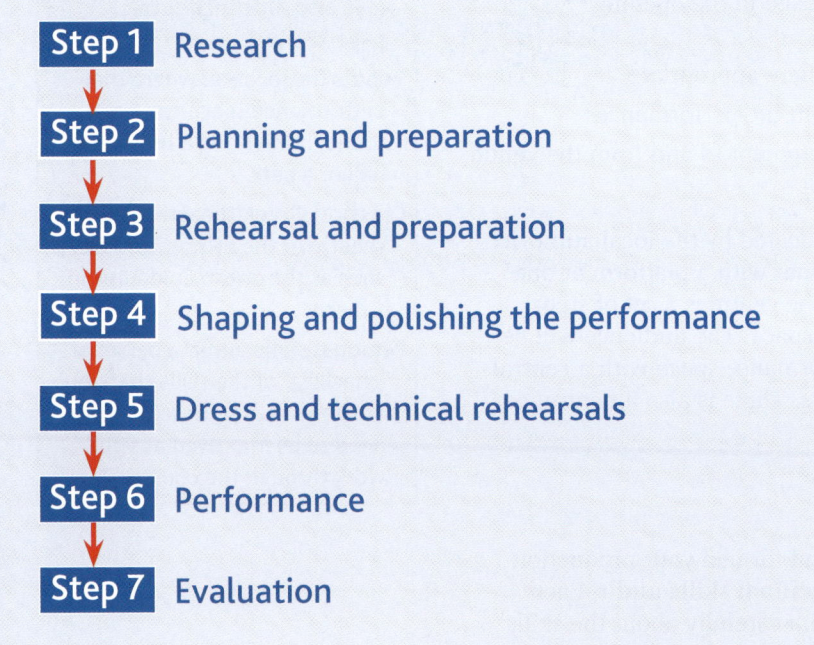

- Step 1 Research
- Step 2 Planning and preparation
- Step 3 Rehearsal and preparation
- Step 4 Shaping and polishing the performance
- Step 5 Dress and technical rehearsals
- Step 6 Performance
- Step 7 Evaluation

UNIT ONE: Skills development

Practice showcase brief 1

1 The Olympics past and present

The Olympics: past and present

As part of a celebration of the Olympic Games, your **production company** is invited to perform to members of your local community on a Friday and Saturday in June.

The content of your showcase performance should be inspired by the various activities, art forms, festivals and celebrations that reflect aspects of the Olympic Games.

The celebration will be held in the local park where an **arena** space has been allocated to stage the final showcase performance. As it is an open-air **venue**, you will be responsible for providing your own technical and design materials where required. A basic portable lighting rig and sound system will be provided by the venue. We look forward to your contribution.

It is expected that you will:

- devise a showcase performance to fit the brief
- research the performance space
- explore the range of performing arts used in the opening ceremonies of Olympic games
- use set, costume, masks and music where appropriate
- use stage management and crew to run the performances
- consider the need to transport all equipment to and from the venue
- consider health and safety at all times.

The performance space that has been allocated by the local authority represents a **classical Greek theatre** format with a platform at one end. Directly in front of the platform at the centre is a set of steps leading to the semicircular performance space. The audience will be arranged around the outside of the performance space with a central aisle to accommodate entrances and exits. There is also an entrance/exit stage left and right.

Getting started

Once you have read the brief carefully and formed your production company you will need to carry out a **personal skills audit**. Each production company member should think carefully about the skills they can offer to the group. Remember that you need to think about all aspects of the possible production. You will need to decide what the group's strengths are. For example you may have some strong actors and dancers as well as a really creative designer or technician. The important thing to remember is that if you work to your strengths you will produce your best work.

Objectives

In this section you will learn:

to develop your performance skills

to build materials for your portfolio.

Key terms

Production company: the group that you will work with to develop the ideas that will be rehearsed and performed; it takes responsibility for all aspects of the production that you are about to undertake.

Arena: an area, surrounded on three sides by seating, in which a performance, entertainment or sporting event takes place (see also **amphitheatre**, page 18).

Venue: the location where the performance space can be found; it might be a theatre, a hall or a park.

Classical Greek theatre: a typical theatre of the 5th century BCE, such as the one in Epidaurus in Greece.

Personal skills audit: a personal 'checklist' of the skills that you are good at and those that will need to be improved as you work through the course.

Chapter 1   The Olympics past and present   17

Having carried out your skills audit and recorded your findings in your portfolio, you are ready to undertake the first practical activity.

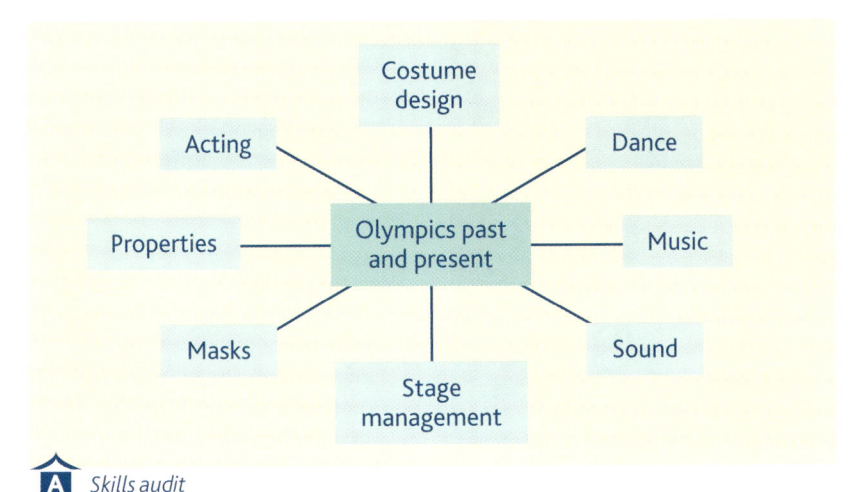

A *Skills audit*

Step 1   Research

The brief clearly states that the final showcase performance is to celebrate the Olympics, past and present (see photos **E** and **F** on page 19 for an example). Your production company will need to research the historical aspects of the theme. If you are not sure where to start then you might use the school library or the internet but remember that it is very important that the research is your own and any notes are written by you and your company.

You should all take responsibility for a particular aspect of the research and prepare a short presentation to the production company. You should prepare each presentation with appropriate materials. You might include selected images, diagrams, original posters created by company members, costume designs, PowerPoint slides and a prepared spoken presentation with notes. Copies of the presentations should be available for all company members for inclusion in the research section of the portfolio. However you must always clearly acknowledge any material that is not your own original work.

Activity

1   Examine the brief

Look at the key words in the brief and identify the possible skill areas with which you might want to work. You can use the suggestions in diagram **A** as a starting point.

You might add other skills or remove some that you are not sure about.

At this stage do not rule anything out. Try to cover all the skills that your company can offer. You may need to research skills that you have not experienced, such as technical aspects of production.

Remember

Look back at the seven steps to success on page 15.

B *A traditional Greek amphitheatre*

C *The opening ceremony for the Beijing Olympics*

Puppeteers at the Beijing Olympics opening ceremony

Remember
You will only be credited with work that you have undertaken yourself or as a member of your production company. Any research downloaded from the internet must be **annotated** and clearly acknowledged.

Key terms
Annotated: printed materials such as scripts, downloaded information and source materials that you have made notes on to assist your understanding when carrying out research during the course. An annotated text will be accepted as part of your portfolio work as it shows that you have considered the content of the text and have some understanding of it.

Amphitheatre: an open-air building based on Greek and Roman architecture, with a central space for the presentation of dramatic or sporting activities.

Paralympics: an international athletic competition for athletes with disabilities.

Cirque du Soleil: a French-Canadian performing arts group famous for their exciting mix of traditional circus skills, mask work, storytelling and original music in performance.

Activity

2 Research the brief

Here are some suggested topics for your research:
- **amphitheatre** design and function
- the origins of the Olympic Games
- the Olympic ideal
- sports included in the original Olympic Games
- the 'modern' Olympic Games
- the **Paralympics**
- stylised movement and dance based on sporting activities (gymnastic floor exercises with ribbons, martial arts)
- costume design
- Greek gods and Mount Olympus
- opening ceremonies
- famous Olympic athletes
- historical events around the Olympics
- female representation at the Olympic Games
- **Cirque du Soleil**.

AQA Examiner's tip
All your research should be included in your portfolio with any comments and personal notes. All of these materials will be important at the **production meetings** and will form the basis of your final choices for the showcase performance.

Chapter 1 The Olympics past and present 19

E Olympic athlete Kelly Sotherton

F A Greek urn showing spear-throwing. Compare with photo E for an idea of Olympics past and present!

Remember that the more colourful and visual your presentation is the more effective it will be in interesting members of your company. Once you have shared your findings choose which to include in your showcase performance.

Your presentations might include:

- the gods discussing the games
- dances based on sports moves
- cheerleader routines.

Examiner's tip

The specification suggests that you should spend approximately 15 hours carrying out your research and planning. This is an indication of how important this aspect of the work is. The better you are prepared, the better the final results will be. It is also worth remembering that everything that you do during the research and planning stages should be kept in your portfolio.

Key terms

Production meetings: meetings where all the company members will discuss issues that arise, record their thoughts and plan the performance. Minutes of these meetings should be dated and kept safely in your portfolio.

Blocking: planning and rehearsal of the moves of the performers and recording them in the stage manager's book.

Choreography: a sequence of dance steps or movements created for performance.

Extension

1 Why not watch extracts from films like *Chariots of Fire*? Look at the way the director uses modern music and slow motion to create excitement as the athletes run. This film also manages to recreate the atmosphere of the early modern Olympics and some of the issues that surrounded them.

There are lots of films that have sport as a theme or have sport as a focus for key scenes. Why not check them out? How many can you think of?

Activity

3 Research the venue

Having carried out your research it will be necessary to either visit the venue or to get details of it from the organisers. You should work to the details given in the brief and draw a plan for your portfolio. This plan should be used when deciding on your designs, **blocking** and **choreography**.

When you have made your plan, place one copy in your portfolio and have copies available at all your rehearsals as a reminder of the performance space.

Step 2 Planning and preparation

The next stage is to hold a production planning meeting and bring together all the ideas that the company have collected and make a **short list** of those that you feel are possible for your company to perform, keeping in mind the chosen audience and venue.

It is always a good idea to have more to work with than you will need for the final performance. This allows you to try things out and make a selection of material based on experience rather than just instinct. It is very important to be realistic and if the running time exceeds the guidelines given in the specification you will need to cut rather than hope that things get faster. The pace of the performance is important but you cannot rely on things speeding up just to allow you to keep pieces in. Make sure that all members of your company have an equal chance to show their skills to best advantage. Everyone in the company will have worked hard and it is only fair that they have the opportunity to show the results of their hard work.

You should present your ideas to your teacher, who will supervise and direct the practical workshops and rehearsals to ensure that you meet the needs of the brief.

Extension

2   Call a production company meeting and discuss a resources list. Decide on a budget for the performance. You will need to list all the materials that you are going to need for costumes and props as well as set if they are appropriate. Why not think about recycling things from other productions? Remember you need to be realistic. Why not ask your teacher for an idea of what might be available to use?

Key terms

Short list: the list of ideas that the production company has decided to include in the final performance – the best ideas uncovered by the research.

Hint

Once you have experience and confidence you will be allowed to work more independently.

When you think about the final performance you should also think about your budget and resources. Think carefully about the cost of any resources that you might need and try to cost the total production.

AQA Examiner's tip

The important thing to keep in mind throughout the whole process is that this is a team effort and you must work to the company's strengths if you are to succeed.

Remember

You will need to be realistic and make sure that you choose carefully.

It is a good idea to refer back to the brief at each stage in the production process.

G Pilot Theatre production meeting

Chapter 1 The Olympics past and present   **21**

If you are considering music as an option you will need to consider creating original pieces that complement the work that you eventually include in your final showcase performance. You can use a range of instruments including woodwind and drums to provide rhythms for dance and drama but equally use modern instruments and recording techniques to provide atmospheric pieces to enhance the different aspects of the performance. You will need to work with all the company members to discuss and plan exactly what is needed.

> **AQA Examiner's tip**
>
> You may have more ideas than you will need for the final performance. Don't worry; it allows more flexibility in shaping the performance. However, be prepared to 'cut' ideas to make the performance more effective.

H *Drummers at the Beijing Olympics opening ceremony*

Extension

3 Observe your dancers as they create a piece of choreography and, using a drum, beat out a rhythm that fits the piece.

This activity should form part of the rehearsal process and will allow you to understand how the performances that your company are involved in can work together.

Activity

4 Try out ideas

Try out some of your ideas with your teacher:

- consider the skills of the group when your final choices are made
- work out the potential length of the pieces
- produce a running order of the material to be included in the final performance.

> **Hint**
>
> The running time of the final performances is important and guidelines are clearly stated in the specification. However it is expected that each production company should not exceed 30 minutes' performance time. This has clear implications for the number of pieces in the final performance.

Step 3 Rehearsal and preparation

Having allocated all the **roles and responsibilities** required of your production company you will need to think about how the final performance will look. At this stage you will need to review all the information you have and make sure that you have met the demands of the original brief. You should call a production meeting in order to plan your rehearsal period.

Activity

5 Hold a production meeting

The purpose of this meeting is to discuss the following:

- Has the company met the demands of the original brief?
- Have all the pieces to be included in the final performance been timed?
- Have all the costumes been designed and are they available for the final rehearsals?
- Have the technical aspects of the performance been met?
- Have the company been rehearsing in a way that will make the transfer of the final performance to the venue as trouble free as possible? Has the performance been rehearsed in an area similar to that of the final performance space?

Having answered all these questions make a list of things to do and check it with your teacher.

This aspect of the work is by far the most difficult but also the most rewarding. You should now have a list of material to be rehearsed and you should have identified who will be allocated roles and responsibilities for all aspects of the rehearsal process. For example, the stage manager should begin to build **the Book**. This will record all the moves and positions of the performers and any technical requirements. The stage manager will need to make careful notes at each rehearsal and make sure that everything in the Book can be understood. The stage manager will be the person who runs the show and needs to be able to work with the performers and the technical team in the dress and technical **runs** as well as in the final performances. However, if the stage manager is ill or unable to be at a rehearsal or performance then the Book must be clear so that the person who takes over can understand it.

If you are a performer you will need to take time to study the part you are to play in the performance whether it is to learn a script, create an improvisation, choreograph a dance sequence or, as a designer, create the costumes and props. The rehearsal process is essential. You will need to consider your relationship with other performers and work out in detail the qualities that you want the final performance to have. Every member of the group should keep in mind the original brief and the target audience as this will have an impact on the way in which you rehearse and prepare the chosen material.

Hint

When you take on roles and responsibilities, you undertake to meet the demands of the jobs that you have been asked to do and meet all the deadlines that have been set.

Key terms

Roles and responsibilities: the jobs that you undertake as part of your production company.

The Book: all the information needed to ensure that the performance goes smoothly; it is kept by the stage manager and is also referred to as the stage copy, the 'bible' or the prompt copy.

Run: a rehearsal or performance that brings every aspect of the piece together; in the dress run, the performers work in their costumes; in a technical run, the technical team rehearses the lighting and sound cues and any special effects.

AQA Examiner's tip

The specification suggests that the rehearsal period should be approximately 30 hours, depending on the size of your company. Keep this in mind when planning your rehearsal schedules if you want to achieve the best results.

Chapter 1   The Olympics past and present

A stage manager at work with their Book

Activity

6 Create the Book

All members of the company should know how to create the Book. Creating the Book is a very important part of the process and must be clear and detailed.

The Book should include:

- all scripts in running order including any descriptions of dance and musical pieces
- all ground plans of the performance space and settings
- blocking details
- props lists
- costume lists
- technical cues
- contact names and numbers
- rehearsal schedules
- performance dates and times
- performance reports including running times
- list of any health-and-safety issues
- things-to-do lists based on events at rehearsals and performances
- records of role allocation.

Each member of the company should take responsibility for one part of the performance and prepare a draft copy of the moves and technical details required.

Remember

You will spend a lot of time in rehearsal and at the end of each session you should record your progress and list things to do in time for the next rehearsal. These notes will be important when you evaluate your work.

Production company meetings should be called on a regular basis to meet and discuss the progress made. Minutes of these meetings are essential and should be kept safely in your portfolio for future reference.

During the rehearsal and preparation period you will be working either as part of a group or as an individual but always as a member of the company led by your teacher. Always remember that the final performance will succeed or fail depending on the overall effort of the company. Everyone involved in the company is important and has a point of view that is valid. Every company member should be prepared to help wherever it is necessary in order to achieve the best results. You should keep detailed records of any decisions made in your portfolio.

Activity

7 Record progress

Throughout the rehearsal period it is important to record your progress and also to encourage others to observe your work. Your teachers will observe your progress and write reports for the final assessments but you should observe other members of your company and write a short observation about them. This doesn't need to be too detailed but should give an idea of how they work and why the contribution they have made to the rehearsal process has been successful. It is also essential that you are positive and supportive in your observations; after all you are expecting the same considerations to be made for you.

You will need to include at least three witness statements in your portfolio.

Extension

4 As part of your preparation, watch a film or TV drama and write a review focusing on a particular performance. Try to say what it is you like or dislike about the performance and why. Start with short written statements and gradually add details as you gain confidence. As you develop the observational skills required, write down your thoughts. You should be prepared to do the same for your own performances and those of other performers in your company.

Key terms

Witness statement: a description of your progress and skills development that can be written by a teacher, parent or friend. Even the caretaker may wish to write about how well you have cleared away after rehearsals!

Remember

The rehearsal period works better if you:

- stick to deadlines and have clear schedules
- rehearse rather than sit around talking
- plan designs and make drafts before deciding on the final look
- always work as a member of the company and are aware of all elements of the production
- are aware of the health-and-safety issues and safe working practices that apply to the activity that you are involved in.

This period of time is always difficult but can be made easier with regular production company meetings so that everyone is aware of any difficulties that may have arisen. A problem shared is a problem halved if not solved. You may have one specific role to play in the final performance but your thoughts and ideas may be useful when observing the rehearsals of others.

As the rehearsal period progresses you will become aware of the equipment, props, costumes and effects that might be required. You should list these and discuss them at the regular production-company meetings. However all members of the company must take responsibility for their own equipment – for example, collecting and returning props and taking care of them, especially in performance.

All members of the company should prepare a physical warm up. For example, if actors choose not to warm up their voice, they could end up with a sore throat at best and a lost voice at worst. The dancers in the company will also need to prepare with a physical warm up in order to avoid injury.

Chapter 1 The Olympics past and present 25

Activity

8 Work out a warm-up programme

Work out a short warm-up programme based on your chosen skill:

- Actors should understand the importance of the voice and how to use it properly. You can either research possible exercises and make a list of those that you like and try them out or you can follow exercises that you have used in class.
- Dancers should work out a series of stretching exercises and basic limbering exercises to warm the muscles.
- Musicians should work out a series of exercises that develop flexibility and stamina.

J *Warming up is important when preparing for a performance*

Activity

9 Design technical aspects

Design elements are important and once you have decided on the content of your performance you should begin to consider the following aspects of production and who will take responsibility for them:

- costume
- props
- set
- sound
- lighting
- stage management
- making of props such as masks
- making up the stage manager's final Book.

AQA Examiner's tip

The making of props, for example, takes time and this has to be built into the preparation period.

Step 4 Shaping and polishing the performance

It is important that you start to 'run' the complete programme and begin to integrate the technical aspects of the performance. Here is a checklist to help you shape and polish your final performance.

- Are the costumes practical and do they fit the performers?
- Is the set workable?
- Are the props practical and fit for purpose?
- Are sound, music and lighting appropriate and do they work well within the context of the overall performance?
- Are the actors and dancers well rehearsed and confident?
- Are you ready for the dress and technical rehearsals at the venue?

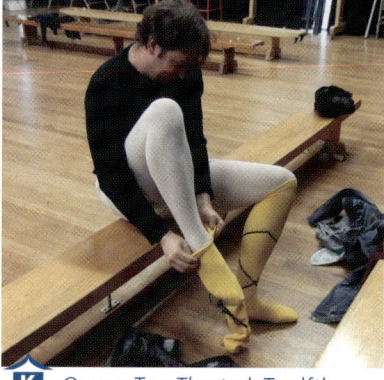

K Orange Tree Theatre's *Twelfth Night* tour, Richmond

Activity

10 Hold a run through

- Prepare for a run through of all the material to be included in the final showcase performance.
- After the run through, each company member should write a short evaluation of what took place.
- The evaluation should state any changes that are to be made before the dress and technical performance and give reasons why.
- Individual members should think about their own contribution and how effective it was. They should discuss any changes that are to be made with other company members. Remember this is team effort and everyone needs to understand the reasons for any changes.

L Dancers practising for their performance

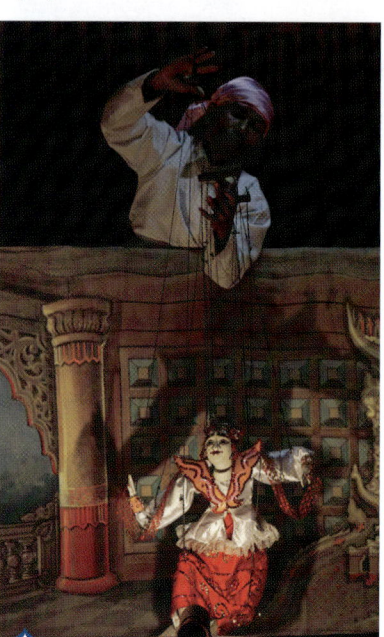

M A puppeteer preparing for performance

Step 5 Dress and technical rehearsals

The dress and technical run-throughs are very important as they bring together all the elements of your final production. To ensure that everything goes according to plan your company needs to be well organised. You should call a production meeting to go over every aspect of the performance.

You will need to check the following before the dress and technical rehearsal:

- Is the performance space set correctly with any props and furniture?
- Are the costumes ready and allocated to the performers?
- Are the technical requirements clearly recorded on the appropriate cue sheets?
- Is the technical equipment working and are any recorded sounds and music ready and available to play?
- Have all the health and safety issues been covered?
- Is the set in place and secure?
- Is the stage manager's Book up to date and ready to use?
- Are the props tables ready and props set according to need – for example, stage right or stage left?
- As the venue is in the open air, have you an alternative performance space in the event of bad weather?

> **AQA Examiner's tip**
>
> It is a good idea to have someone watch the technical and dress rehearsals. You could ask other members of your performing arts group to act as audience and make notes. This will give you an idea of how the performance works with an audience and also any problems that need to be dealt with before the final performance.

> **Hint**
>
> It is sometimes useful to carry out the dress rehearsal in front of an audience in order to get an idea of how the showcase works.

If you are going to perform away from your usual rehearsal space you will need to organise the move to the venue. There are a number of questions to answer, for example:

- Who is responsible for transporting the set, props, costumes and technical equipment including musical instruments if they are required?
- How are you and the company going to travel to the venue?
- What is the cost of transport to and from the venue?

These are important questions and the answers should form an important part of your portfolio notes.

Step 6 Performance

Provided you have worked hard and rehearsed well, you should be able to present your performance with confidence. Remember, provided you have allocated the specific roles and responsibilities everyone will be working as a member of the team. Even when people are carrying out their roles and responsibilities in a live performance, things can go wrong. A cue can be missed, a prop may not work or an entrance may be delayed because someone is waiting in the wrong place. However the important thing is to carry on.

Whether you are a performer or a technician, the important thing is to feel that you have managed to create a piece of work that shows your skills off to best advantage. As an actor, dancer or musician you will have rehearsed and warmed up appropriately before the performance, lines will have been learnt, choreography will be secure. As a technician, you will need to have lighting and sound cue sheets ready to follow and all health and safety issues will have been considered.

Check lists of roles and responsibilities are useful to have around the performance area as a reminder for company members. Your teacher will have checked that you have everything in place.

Did you know ??????

In the theatre, performers are always in the venue 35 minutes before the performance starts. Many performers are there much earlier. They have to get ready, warm up their bodies and voices, apply make-up, get into costume, check their props and settle their nerves.

N *Rigging the lights at the King's Theatre, Southsea*

Activity

11 Clear up

At the end of the performance you will need to clear up by:
- striking the set
- returning props and costumes
- derigging and returning equipment
- clearing dressing rooms
- loading the van
- checking all the technical equipment lists.

AQA Examiner's tip

It is worth remembering that your teacher is assessing you. You need to demonstrate your ability to:
- work as a member of a team
- carry out tasks and perform effectively in your specific skills area during the performance
- take responsibility for everything that you need for the performance, such as costume, props, equipment, musical instruments and cue sheets.

Having completed the first of the practice briefs you are ready to begin to build your skills further. Make sure that all your research, scripts, inspirational materials, designs, cue sheets, minutes of meetings and evaluations and assessment sheets are safely placed in your portfolio as these will form a very important part of the work to be assessed in Unit 1.

Step 7 Evaluation

Evaluation is an essential part of any performance. It is very important that you understand the process you have gone through.

You should look back over everything that you have recorded in the portfolio and use this as the basis of your final evaluation. You will need to update your skills audit and carry it forward to the next brief.

Evaluation of your own work
- Reread your original skills audit sheet.
- Decide what you have improved, how and why.
- Decide what you have learned and give examples.
- Decide which disciplines you would like to try next time – for example, an actor might benefit from a design or technical activity.

Evaluation of planning and research
- Write about your own responsibilities.
- Did the performance meet the demands of the brief?
- How effective was the research that you did?
- Consider any difficulties that arose and how you overcame them.

Evaluation of practical activities
- Were the rehearsal techniques effective?
- How could they be improved next time?
- Which practical activities did you find most useful? These might, for example, include performance games or warm ups.
- Can you identify the relationship between your own practical work and processes and those of the professional industry?

Knowledge and understanding of work-related aspects
- Do you understand what it might be like to work in the professional performing arts industry?
- Can you make constructive comments on your own and others' work?

You might find that you will already have made some comments in other areas of the evaluation process that could be included in this section. It is worth checking because you can't be given credit for them if they are not included.

Remember
- Give yourself plenty of time to prepare for the performance.
- Don't leave everything to the last minute.
- Enjoy the performance!

Evaluation of your own and others' work

This is an important part of the evaluation. You will need to think about how you and other members of the production company worked together.

- Consider the work of other company members and write short evaluations of their contribution to the final performance.
- Think about your performance and how it contributed to the overall effectiveness of the performance. For example, was your characterisation well considered? Were you clear about what you had to do? What went well and what might you change next time you perform?
- Think about the teamwork that took place during the rehearsal period. How important was it and why?
- Highlight one or two aspects of the process that you feel worked well and give details.
- Highlight one or two aspects of the process that you feel could be improved next time and say why.

Having completed the evaluation process you should have lots of important information to put into the portfolio. You should refer back to all the work that you have done as you progress through the course. The process will form the basis of all the work that you do in future.

As you approach your next practice brief don't forget what you need to develop. It is important to work on your strengths but also remember to try out new skills next time around. Remember – the important thing is that you build your confidence in the skills that you choose to follow. Always be aware of others in your group as you work towards the final externally set brief.

It is important to meet and evaluate your performance

Practice showcase brief 2

2 Pantomime

The history of theatre

The regional Arts Council invites your production company to take part in this event.

Your theme is pantomime.

The content should be suitable for the whole community and should reflect historical aspects and contemporary interpretations.

You will perform twice in your local theatre and tour in one or more junior schools of your choice in December.

We look forward to your contribution.

Objectives

In this section you will learn:

the history of pantomime and the nature of its audience

pantomime style and production conventions

skills and techniques of pantomime in performance.

A Aladdin *at the Everyman Theatre, Cheltenham*

Step 1 Research

The theme is pantomime but the brief includes the celebration of the history of theatre. Where does pantomime fit into the history of theatre? Answering this question will immediately enable you to score marks for research because you will have to look at different styles of theatre in different countries and in different historical periods to show how this very British tradition of popular entertainment came into existence.

> *Pantomime is traditional Christmas entertainment of the British Empire*
>
> Oxford Companion to the Theatre

AQA Examiner's tip

Don't just download pages from the internet. It gains you no marks. **Annotate** any printed research to explain how the information is useful or relevant to your own progress.

Key terms

Annotate: summarise, in your own words, notes that give further explanation of printed material.

Activity

1 Present your research

Create a two-minute PowerPoint presentation about the origins of pantomime for the rest of your group. This is excellent evidence for your Unit 1 portfolio to show that you have explored and understood a range of theatrical **genres** from different countries and historical periods.

Key terms

Genre: a style of theatre, such as a play, musical, opera, ballet, pop concert, comedy or pantomime.

Can you find evidence of the influences shown in diagram **B**?

Origins of pantomime

- Commedia dell'Arte
- Harlequinade
- Troupes of Dancers
- Music Hall
- Melodrama
- Burlesque
- Variety artists
- Punch and Judy
- Unlicensed theatres of the 18th century

B *Origins of pantomime*

AQA Examiner's tip

The best evidence you can provide is written reviews of your own trips to the theatre. If you can meet, work with or interview professionals in the industry you will be rewarded for contextual understanding of work-related aspects.

Did you know ??????

For some people, pantomime is the only form of live theatrical entertainment they have ever seen. The annual Christmas pantomime is popular in most regional theatres and important for box-office takings. Its target audiences are families and whole community audiences.

C *Have you been to see a traditional pantomime at your local theatre?*

Chapter 2   Pantomime   33

Diagram **D** shows some of the traditional aspects of pantomime that your research should have revealed.

Audience expectations

- Popular references
- Song
- Christmas
- Limelight
- Audience participation
- Glamour
- Fairytales
- Comic relief
- Music
- Famous TV/sports/pop stars in the cast

D Audience expectations

E The poster advertising the Everyman's pantomime

Activity

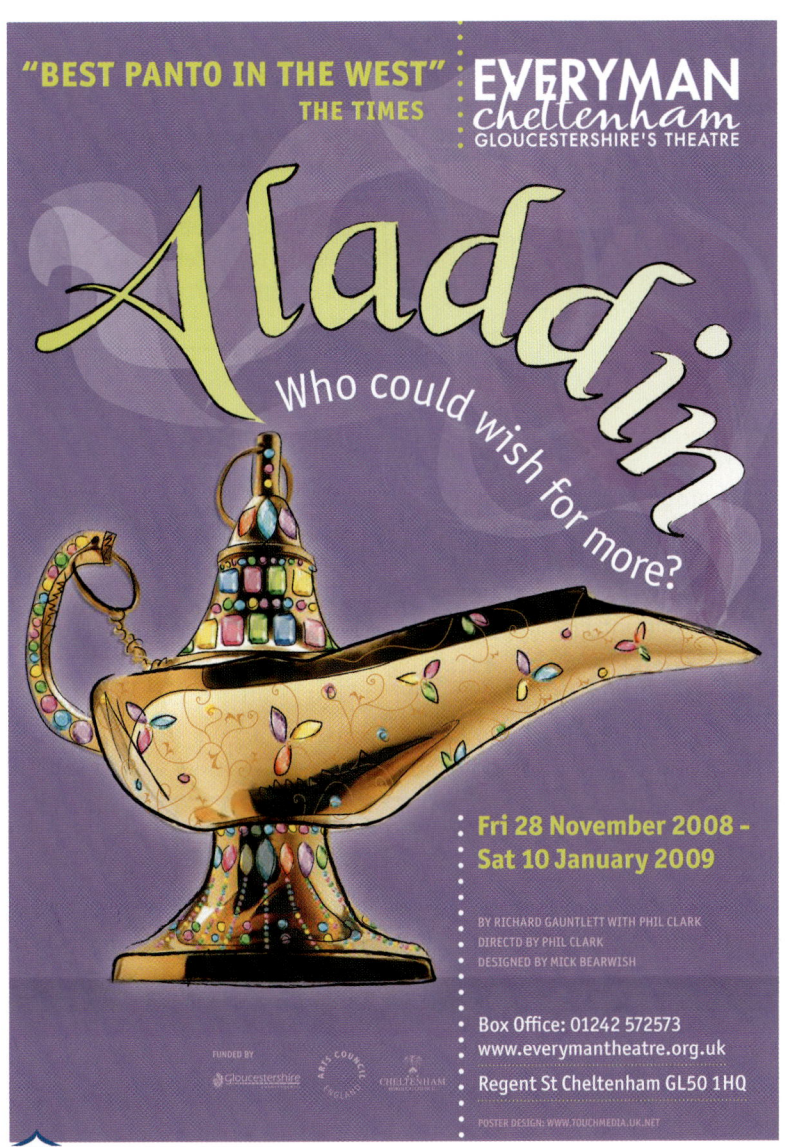

2 Identify your audience

Conduct a survey of the students in your class to find out if they have been to the theatre. What did they see? What genre was it? How old were they? Did they go with their friends or family? Why did they enjoy it? What did they expect?

Key terms

Popular references: words, phrases or songs that a modern audience will recognise and identify with.

Audience participation: moments when the audience takes part in the action and contributes to the performance on stage.

Did you know ??????

The Oldham Coliseum has annually presented a very traditional pantomime whereas Theatr Clwyd has developed a style of rock and roll pantomime that is also very successful and popular. What style of pantomime does your local theatre produce?

AQA Examiner's tip

Visit, measure, photograph and make notes of technical and front-of-house information in your proposed performance spaces. This is valuable research, essential later for designing and rigging purposes.

Did you know ??????

Professional theatres provide visiting companies with a full technical specification of all their performance spaces. Why not ask your local theatre for a specification?

At this point, you need to research the spaces in which you will be performing. You can assume that your local theatre is well equipped with all the facilities and equipment that you need to perform your show. There will be few technical limits on what you might want to do there. The constraints on your production will come from elsewhere:

- **Budget**: do you have the financial resources to design and transport a show suitable for different spaces and venues?
- **The size of the space**: how does the theatre space compare to the size of the primary school space? Can you design a show big enough for the theatre but small enough for the primary school?
- **The shape of the spaces and their relationship with their audiences**: few primary schools have proscenium arches or raised stages. Will you have to work in the round or on a thrust?
- **Portable rostra**: will you need flexible staging in the school?
- **Technical facilities**: a primary school will not have the sound or lighting systems of a theatre. Can you design a successful show for both venues?
- **Lights and sound**: what can you provide if the primary school venue has none?
- **Transport**: you will have to design a show that you can get in and out of the theatre to transfer to local primary schools. Your set might fit in the space but will it fit in a transit van? How else might you transport it?
- **Time**: how much time will you have to get in, perform and get out of each venue? You must plan for this.
- **Health and safety**: consider the issues with regard to your company and their audience.

Did you know ??????
Rebecca Ryan, who plays Debbie Gallagher in the TV programme Shameless, is a world-class Irish dancer. Most actors are multiskilled. They have to be, in a very competitive profession.

AQA Examiner's tip
In a contemporary interpretation, Aladdin might be a break dancer, rapper, DJ or skateboarder who finds a genie in an old mobile phone.

Activity

3 Carry out a skills audit

Make a **skills audit** of what talents you have as a group. You will probably already have some experienced dancers, actors and singers but do you have anyone with technical skills such as sound, set, lighting or stage management? Have you anyone with unusual skills such as break dancing or tumbling? Who can organise the publicity, marketing and box office? You will all need to work as a team and develop new skills to add to your main role.

Step 2 Planning and preparation

- You might wish to cast your performers by audition.
- You will need to consider the skills and techniques expected of pantomime's **stock characters**.
- You will also need to appoint your technical and backstage crews.
- How do professional companies do this?

Key terms
Skills audit: a detailed check or inspection of what skills you have as an individual and as a group.

Stock character: a stereotype that the audience expects to see.

Step 3 Rehearsal and preparation

You must choose, create or adapt your script:

- There are many pantomime scripts available from publishers which are subject to copyright. If you choose a published script you may have to pay a fee.
- You could adapt a script to suit your company and audience.
- You may be able to devise your own show through improvisation.
- Your teacher may write or provide a script.

Try to include some of the traditional conventions of pantomime in your showcase.

> **Hint**
> - Use your teacher! Your teacher is there to assist, direct and facilitate your work.
> - Take lots of photos!
> - Be realistic about your time and capabilities.
> - Learn from other people – adults and your peers.

Pantomime conventions

Proscenium arch	The Dame	Pained backdrops
Two-dimensional scenery	Perspective	Special effects
	Floodlights	Fairy godmother
Principle boy	Ugly sisters	Outrageous stage props
Flying machinery	Pantomine animals	Magic
Slapstick comedy	Clowning	Silly wigs
	Extravagant costume	

F *Pantomime conventions*

Once the show has been cast and responsibilities allocated the rehearsal process can begin:

- Produce a rehearsal schedule.
- A strict code of attendance at rehearsals must be applied.
- A high level of professional conduct is essential.
- Actors should know their lines. There is no excuse.
- Professionals say that there is no easy way to learn lines but that the more you learn the easier it becomes.
- During early blocking actors may wish to make notes in their script on attitudes, behaviour, motivation and their movements on set.
- You cannot rehearse action if you are reading a script.
- Songs, dance routines and set pieces should be rehearsed separately and brought to full rehearsals in a polished state.

G *What pantomime conventions can you see here?*

> **Remember**
> - You are working professionally now, to deadlines.
> - Missing a rehearsal is not the same as missing homework.
> - Other actors are relying on you and their work will be affected by yours.
> - The tickets have been sold and the audience expects!

Step 4 Shaping and polishing the performance

How you shape and polish your performance or technical input will depend on your commitment, creativity and capacity in your designated roles. You will have to consider the following aspects of your skills.

Performance skills

- **Acting**:
    - stereotypical or stock characters and direct address to the audience
    - asides and solo set pieces
    - melodrama, sentimentality, cross-dressing and ham acting.
- **Singing**:
    - traditional, seasonal and contemporary songs
    - big solos and sentimental duets
    - comedy routines and big production numbers.
- **Dancing**:
    - solos, duets and production numbers
    - choreography and dance direction.
- **Live music**:
    - traditional or modern
    - orchestra in the pit or band on stage
    - melodramatic accompaniment.
- **Variety acts**: whatever skills the performers may bring would meet audience expectations.

Physical design skills

- **Set design**:
    - building, painting and dressing the set
    - fairytale locations and painted backdrops.
- **Properties**:
    - identify, list, acquire or make
    - larger than life for comic effect.
- **Costume**:
    - identify, acquire or design and make
    - outrageous and colourfully exaggerated.
- **Make-up and hair**:
    - design and apply
    - stereotypically exaggerated to combat the footlights.
- **Masks or puppets**:
    - identify, design and make
    - anything from a pantomime horse to *Sooty and Sweep*.

H Musicians need to rehearse their stage performance too

I Make-up is an important part of the design

Technical design and management skills

- **Lighting**:
  - design, rig, patch, colour, focus, plot and control
  - conventionally based on footlights and spotlights
  - the conventions of music hall and melodrama are expected.
- **Sound**:
  - identify, design, record, plot, rig, mix, test and control
  - live or recorded, realistic or comic effects
  - are you using hand, head, directional microphones or none at all?
- **Stage management**:
  - organise rehearsals, create the prompt copy, rig and set the props
  - special effects, stage traps, pyrotechnics and flying machinery
  - manage the crew, cue the actors and call the show
  - health and safety on stage is a major responsibility for stage management.

Production skills

- **Front-of-house management**:
  - draw a seating plan for each venue
  - organise, produce and sell all the tickets for each venue
  - collect revenue and run the box office for each venue
  - audience access, catering, health and safety at each venue.
- **Marketing and publicity**:
  - decide the design theme, timescale and budget for the advertising campaign
  - posters and flyers must be designed, printed and distributed
  - organise press releases and photo opportunities.

Step 5 Technical and dress rehearsals

Technical rehearsal

The technical rehearsal is for the benefit primarily of the stage crew, sound and lighting control.

From this point the stage manager is in total control of the show. What happens backstage, in the wings and on the control desks is just as important as what happens on stage. Cues and timings must be tested, rehearsed and adjusted if necessary.

- Actors must be aware of technical, set, furniture and property cues.
- Costumes may be used only if they have issues for the stage or technical crew, such as magic wands or radio microphones fitted into costumes.
- Full scenes may not be run if there are no technical cues to rehearse and the full cast may not be called.
- The health and safety of actors, crew and audience must be considered.

J *Technical rehearsals are important for the whole production company*

Dress rehearsal

- This is the first full run through of the finished show as the audience will see it.
- It is the final opportunity for adjustments to cues.
- It is the final opportunity for the director to give feedback to the actors.
- An invited audience will be essential for interaction and reaction.
- The striking of the set at the end must consider the need for storage and transportation to other venues.

Step 6 Performance

Now is the chance to put your skills development to the test. Having a live audience should improve your **focus** and your performance. The stage manager calls the company to prepare; the audience arrives and the tension mounts backstage; the stage manager calls **beginners** and the show begins.

When you have to work in different venues:

- you will need to consider the problems of transferring a show
- you will need transport for the cast, crew, set, costumes, props and technical equipment
- there may be a technical **get-out** and **get-in** followed by a technical run through and dress rehearsal
- the crew must recheck everything and the actors must be ready for performance.

Step 7 Evaluation

By now you should know what is required in an evaluation:

- What new techniques and skills have you developed?
- How has your knowledge and understanding of theatre style and conventions improved?
- How did you respond to feedback from your teacher?
- What did you set out to do?
- How did you propose to do it?
- How did you implement your proposals?
- What problems did you encounter?
- How did you overcome them?
- What did you learn in the process?
- What would you do differently? Why?
- What did you think of your achievement?
- Were you successful?
- How do you know?
- What did your audience think?
- What did your critics have to say?

AQA Examiner's tip

Remember that each audience is different. They will react to different lines and moments in performance. With experience, you will learn to work with and for your audience. Focus and concentrate on your role and responsibilities. Evaluation of your audience response is important in Unit 1 (portfolio) and Unit 2 (showcase performance).

Key terms

Focus: full concentration on the task in hand.

Beginners: the people required in the first scene.

Get-in: rigging or putting up the set and lights for a production.

Get-out: striking the set and rigging at the end of a production.

AQA Examiner's tip

The practical tasks of get-in and get-out are very important not just as preparation for performance but for the work-related section of your Unit 1 portfolio. Take photographs and record all of your experiences!

Remember

- A live show takes on a life of its own.
- Performers, technicians, operators and crew are all part of the live show.
- Working as a team is essential.
- Taking personal responsibility is essential.
- Things will go wrong! How you cope is a measure of your professionalism.
- Be your own greatest critic but give yourself credit where it's due!

Practice showcase brief 3

3 Every child matters

Every child matters

The school governors invite your production company to perform theatre in education at a school assembly.

The theme is 'every child matters'.

The content and style should reflect your choice of issue and age of target audience.

All technical and design elements will be the responsibility of the company.

You may wish to provide introductory and support material for teachers and students.

We look forward to your contribution.

Objectives

In this section you will learn:

the origins of theatre in education (TIE)

TIE style and production conventions

skills and techniques of TIE in performance.

A A poster for the play *Family Business* performed by the M6 Theatre Company

Key terms

Theatre in education (TIE): a show developed around an educational topic or debate.

Step 1 Research

The brief demands a style of theatre that uses entertainment to inform and educate its audience. Most forms of theatre do this to some extent but three particular forms of theatre practice have contributed to what we now call **theatre in education**:

- didactic theatre – Bertolt Brecht
- forum theatre – Augustus Boal
- theatre in education – the Belgrade Theatre and others.

Your teacher will introduce you to these important theatre practitioners and will direct your research. You should be able to work on some of their ideas in class to develop skills in their style of theatre and to give you the knowledge and understanding to conduct your research with confidence.

There are companies that specialise in producing theatre to be performed in schools (for example, Cragrats, M6 and Activ8). Such productions often have drama workshops attached and may involve the pupils in the performance itself. The performances are often designed with particular aspects of the curriculum in mind. Some link their work to a particular Key Stage, whilst others design various projects for different ages. Theatre in education productions are also especially adapted for touring, making them flexible enough to perform well in school settings.

Carry out a skills audit.

- What skills do you have in your group?
- What skills do you need for this style of theatre?
- Can you use, adapt or develop your existing skills?
- Do you need to develop new skills?
- What skills will you, personally, use and develop for this project?

Activity

1 Identify your audience

Research your audience profile by: age, gender, ethnicity, social class.

- What kind of school do they attend?
- Where is it?
- What are their interests and aspirations?
- What would be the best way of engaging them?

How would you gather this information?

- By direct approach to the headteacher.
- By speaking to the school governors.
- Through internet research.
- From the school brochure.
- Through personal interviews.
- Through questionnaires…?

AQA Examiner's tip

Record carefully what you do, what you learn and how you intend to use this information. This is important for choosing or devising your performance piece and for the research and work-related sections of your portfolio.

Activity

2 Research the agencies

Through your research make a list of agencies (Childline, Connexions, Relateen) which exist to help children and how children are expected to use them. Survey some of your target audience to find out how many of these agencies they are aware of and whether they have used any. Discuss the results with responsible teachers or governors. Use the results to help decide what goes into your show and make sure you record them in your portfolio. This can be high-level work if done carefully.

Chapter 3 Every child matters

Step 2 Planning and preparation

What does 'every child matters' (ECM) mean? It means every child is entitled to:

- be healthy
- stay safe
- enjoy and achieve
- make a positive contribution
- achieve economic wellbeing.

These are referred to as the entitlements in the rest of the chapter.

It is a government policy you can research on the web:

- it applies to all public services, not just education
- you should have a school policy that you can read
- there will be a teacher responsible, whom you can interview
- some schools have a student counsellor
- the school governors are responsible and will be very keen to discuss these entitlements with you, not just to give their views but to listen to yours.

A **stage crew** of technicians might be responsible for **teching** the whole show.

Step 3 Rehearsal and preparation

There are many TIE companies working throughout the country. From your research you will have learned that their work is well published and easily accessible on the internet. You will probably have seen one or more productions in your school. Which companies are active in your area?

B Rehearsing together is essential

AQA Examiner's tip

It is easy to waste valuable time reading and printing documents. Gather information and images that you can use in a PowerPoint presentation as part of the background to your show. Select and organise information that will have a high impact on your audience (a high-level portfolio activity). Ask pastoral and special needs teachers to help you in this.

Hint

Find a dramatically simple and effective way of illustrating what each of the ECM entitlements means and why they are important.

AQA Examiner's tip

Your group could split into smaller groups, each taking responsibility for one ECM entitlement. If each group aims to produce a five- to ten-minute a piece, you have very tight control of your overall running time and each group must be tightly focused to get its message across.

Key terms

Stage crew: the stage management and sound and lighting technicians.

Teching: the technical management of the whole show undertaken by the stage crew.

Did you know ??????

Most TIE productions are followed by audience workshops, interaction or planned worksheets with further resources to assist student learning. Most TIE company websites contain examples of post-performance resources.

It would be ideal if you could time this project to coincide with a TIE visit to your school. You could contact the visiting company in advance and tell it what you are doing. Ask if you can discuss its working methods with it and use its show as a case study for your portfolio.

- How many people does it employ?
- Where does it get its funding?
- Where is it based for rehearsal?
- How does it decide on its projects?
- How does it create its performance pieces?
- How does it market its shows?

You might be surprised at the extent to which it is prepared to help you but, after all, it is in the education business!

> **AQA Examiner's tip**
>
> This work should be recorded as contextual work-related activity as well as research and skills development. See or talk to professional practitioners of theatre in education if you can. Professional influences can provide you with high-level portfolio evidence.

Activity

3 Create a production company

Imagine that you are a professional TIE company. What is your company name? Design a company logo. How will you market your new show?

Activity

4 Allocate roles and responsibilities

Allocate administrative and production responsibilities in your new company. In TIE companies, performers always take on an extra production or technical role.

> **AQA Examiner's tip**
>
> This work is very important for the sections of your portfolio where so many students find it difficult to score marks: contextual work-related comments and evaluation of others' work.

Step 4 Shaping and polishing the performance

Are you going to use an existing script or devise your own? What are the advantages and disadvantages of each approach?

- You could simply use an existing production that meets the requirements of the brief. There are many published plays and musicals that deal with ECM issues. (For example, *Blood Brothers*, *Featherboy* or even *The Wizard of Oz*!)
- There are many scripts available from publishers or on the internet (for example, Samuel French), which might be suitable for your needs or which you could easily borrow from or adapt for your piece.
- You could brainstorm ideas based on your own research to come up with a theme on which you all agree as a group. You will then need to agree about how you would present that theme to your target audience. You would need to structure your piece to fit the time, space and audience for which you are preparing to perform.
- You could create your own **devised production** through improvisation once you have decided on a theme.
- What have you learned from your research about the way that professional companies work?

Are you going to include all five entitlements, from page 41, in your piece? Are you going to devise for each entitlement separately or have a central running narrative or structure?

> **AQA Examiner's tip**
>
> The brainstorm and improvisation process can be very time consuming and students often find it very difficult to agree. Don't let the process become a competition in which you try to impose your ideas over others. You must be prepared to accept other people's ideas, follow others' suggestions and take direction from your peers. Recognising a good idea is clear evidence of professional conduct and you should record it as such in your portfolio.

Create a central character as a focus for the action. This character can then go on a 'journey' in which things happen to him, some bad and some good. These things may each take the form of a scene, each one illustrating one of the lessons that you want the audience to learn or think about. Scenes can be linked by different storytelling devices. Discuss with your teacher the medieval miracle play *Everyman*, which is an **allegory** for the human race. Could you have a central character to represent 'every child' and then construct five scenes to show how each of the entitlements matters in that child's life?

Here are some examples of popular entertainment genres that you might come up with in a brainstorming session:

- a computer game, for example, Tomb Raider or Super Mario Brothers
- a game show, for example *The Weakest Link* or *Deal or no Deal*
- a reality TV show, for example *The X Factor* or *Big Brother*
- every child on a journey through life
- Dorothy on her search for the Emerald City in *The Wizard of Oz*
- *Mother Courage and Her Children* (a piece by Brecht)
- Red Riding Hood going into the woods (a forum piece).

From your skills audit you will know what skills you have and your group has:

- Are you going to work as a whole class or split into as many as five groups?
- Play to your strengths to give your show professional polish but be aware of the need to learn new skills and develop existing ones.
- Your teacher knows what you can do and what you have learned and will give you feedback on your targets and development.
- What technical aids such as lights, sound, props, set or projections will you use?

Music

Are you going to include music, which is always an important aspect of TIE?

- Recorded background or incidental music to create atmosphere or accompany action (melodrama).
- Original music composed by a member of your group and played live as part of the show.
- Traditional songs or rhymes that the audience will recognise as representing typical situations or characters.
- Pop songs, either contemporary or classics, which fit the action or carry an appropriate narrative or message that fits the action.
- Edited or amended popular songs in which the lyrics have been changed to carry a very different message from the original for great dramatic effect. This technique is particularly effective if the song is normally accompanied by recognisable actions. For example, 'YMCA' can easily become 'ASBO' or 'GNVQ' and 'Favourite Things' from *The Sound of Music* can be used to carry almost any narrative. Look at how *Mamma Mia* has used these devices so successfully.

> **Key terms**
>
> **Devised production**: a performance piece that has been created by adapting and combining ideas and extracts from other sources through workshops and improvisation.
>
> **Allegory**: the use of simple symbolic characters or stories to explain and illustrate a more complex idea.

> **AQA Examiner's tip**
>
> Agree on an idea and then stick to it.

> **AQA Examiner's tip**
>
> Use a popular entertainment genre to give your piece structure.

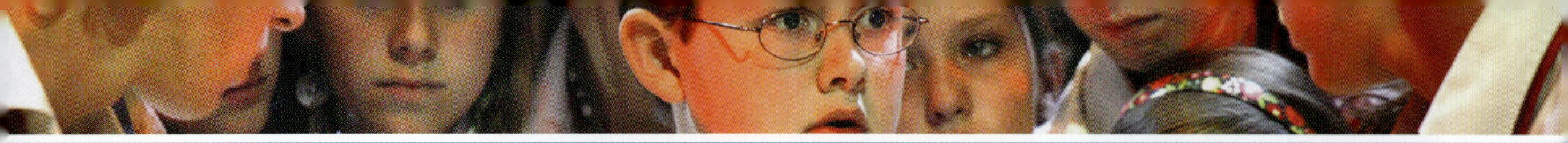

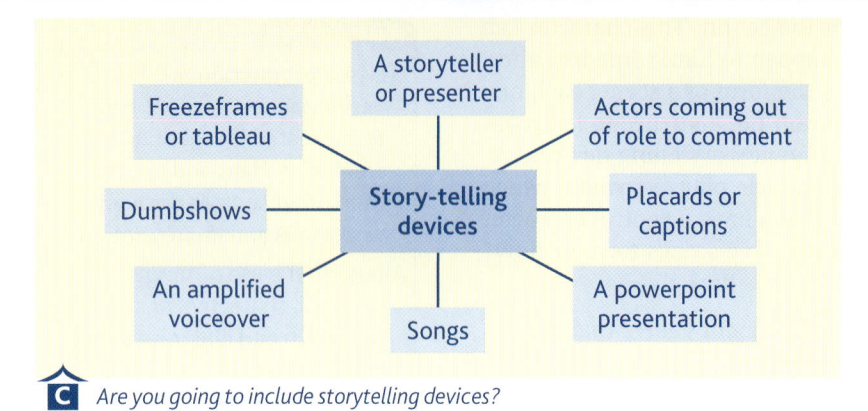

Story-telling devices:
- Freezeframes or tableau
- A storyteller or presenter
- Actors coming out of role to comment
- Dumbshows
- Placards or captions
- An amplified voiceover
- Songs
- A powerpoint presentation

C *Are you going to include storytelling devices?*

Storytelling devices

There are many dramas which use these techniques, some very old and others more modern. They come from different theatrical traditions and use different staging and presentational techniques.

- Many ancient Greek plays use a chorus to tell the story of a character's 'journey'.
- The medieval morality play of *Everyman* personifies human virtues and vices as the friends or enemies of 'Everyman'.
- Do you remember how Pinocchio's nose grew whenever he told a lie?

The German playwright and director Bertholt Brecht developed a whole style of modern theatre which is devoted to 'teaching' the audience:

- He used projections as backdrops to action on stage.
- He used a storyteller to move scenes on quickly to save time.
- He used the storyteller and the actors to comment on what was happening to make sure the audience 'got the message'.
- He allowed actors to come out of role to tell the audience what was happening to the character they were playing.
- He used songs between scenes to tell parts of the story.
- He sometimes invited the audience to be part of the action and, as a group, to play the part of a character.

Did you know ??????

The NT Connections scripts commissioned by the National Theatre and published by Methuen offer a wonderfully diverse range of one-hour plays that address teenage problems from their viewpoint. There is a very modern musical for young actors called *Featherboy*, about a self-conscious teenager who lacks confidence, which uses a variety of techniques to illustrate many of the 'every child matters' issues. You may also wish to look at *Coram Boy*.

AQA Examiner's tip

You will study Brecht if you follow a theatre-based course in further education and any research you do now will be excellent Unit 1 portfolio work and preparation for further study in Unit 3 and beyond.

D *A scene from the National Theatre production of* Feather Boy

Activity

5 **Participate in a workshop**

Ask your teacher to prepare some lessons and workshops to explore some of these texts and methods as part of your skills development and planning and preparation for performance. Make sure you keep a written and photographic record of what you do for your portfolio.

Step 5 Dress and technical rehearsals

- You will need to plan carefully for your assembly. Your show will have to fit into a timetabled slot and be performed on your school stage.
- You could present one piece covering all five entitlements.
- You could focus at length on just one entitlement.
- You could create five 10-minute pieces on each entitlement to be shown in consecutive assemblies.
- Rehearsals should focus on producing a polished piece that is targeted at your audience for maximum impact in the time that you have.
- You should know exactly what technical facilities and what technical support you have available.
- Use your facilities to their best advantage.

Step 6 Performance

Refer back to the performance guidelines in Briefs 1 and 2 (in chapters 1 and 2), where you were performing for the general public. Sometimes, it is very difficult for students to perform to an audience of their peers.

You must be very disciplined. One of the most important requirements of an actor is **courage**.

Be brave. If you are convinced of your performance then you will be convincing!

Step 7 Evaluation

- At every stage in your process you will need feedback from your teacher or peers on your progress.
- You must show in your portfolio how you have responded to feedback.
- How did your audience respond to your piece?
- How do you know?
- Invite written feedback through a questionnaire.
- Evaluate your own performance.
- Invite your peers to evaluate your performance and evaluate theirs.

AQA Examiner's tip

Show in your portfolio how the development of your ideas has been informed by these professional influences. This should include evidence of work-related knowledge as you use techniques learned from professional theatre. If you have seen shows using these techniques then your evaluation of their effectiveness will be important in both the work-related and evaluation sections of your portfolio.

E *Preparation is essential*

UNIT TWO

4 Final showcase performance

Objectives
In this section you will learn:

- to prepare for the final showcase performance
- to prepare for moderation.

The brief for the final showcase performance will be set by AQA and will build on the practical work that you carried out in Unit 1. The final showcase performance will be moderated by a visiting moderator appointed by AQA.

You will work as part of a production company in the same way you did for the practice showcase briefs. Follow the seven steps to success and make sure that you record everything that you do.

You will work as part of a production company and create a showcase performance highlighting your chosen skills area. Your teacher has an important role to play in the process, supervising your progress and offering advice in the role of commissioner of the brief. Your teacher will have the final decision on the content of the showcase and will allow your company to perform to its strengths.

It is expected that you will:

- use your experience and skills to devise a showcase performance to fit the brief
- explore a range of performance styles and genres suitable for the theme and the target audience
- prepare a written outline of what you intend to include in the showcase
- explore a range of suitable venues
- use set and costume, where appropriate
- consider the technical equipment and props necessary for performing the final showcase, including lighting and sound
- use stage management and crew to run the performance
- consider health-and-safety aspects at all times.

Your teacher will issue you with the showcase performance brief and explain what you are required to do. You should review the work that you have been involved in so far and think carefully about the performing arts disciplines that you would like to present as part of the final showcase.

Activity

1 Read the showcase brief

Read the brief carefully and call a production company meeting to discuss what is expected:

- all company members must make notes
- assign roles and responsibilities for the planning process.

■ What you have to do

The first section of the brief sets out what you have to do and what is expected from you and your production company.

AQA Examiner's tip
All the work that you do in preparation for the final showcase performance should be included in your portfolio.

Chapter 4 Final showcase performance

Starter activity

Work out what you have to do

Read the 'what you have to do' section of the brief with your teacher and highlight the most important parts of the instructions:

- hold production meetings
- carry out research
- present your ideas to your teacher, who will act as commissioner
- consider the roles and responsibilities needed for your proposed showcase
- choose the appropriate skills to develop and rehearse
- keep detailed records of the process.

AQA Examiner's tip

The individual briefs section sets out very clearly what you must do to achieve the best results. Keep a copy of the brief safely in your portfolio so that you can refer to it throughout the process.

You will see that the brief focuses on three phases:

- planning and research
- performance
- evaluation.

All three are essential in order to meet the requirements of the showcase performance. The 'seven steps to success' that you followed in the practice briefs should be followed here to ensure that you cover all that is needed to complete the work required of the showcase performance. At this point, you should refresh your memory by looking back over your portfolio.

It is also important to work through the brief carefully. When you have chosen your skills area, read the section titled 'individual briefs' as this gives specific instructions to you as a performer, designer, technician or stage manager.

A A pupil from Bishop's College, Gloucester, adjusting a light

Assessment criteria

The final section of the brief is a copy of the assessment criteria and your teacher will explain how this works. You will be allocated marks for the following three areas:

- skills development and professional conduct
- final performance/design
- evaluation of own work.

You need to look carefully at the assessment grid because it sets out very clearly what is expected and how to achieve the best results. As you will see, the grid is divided into three main areas:

- Skills development and professional conduct: this takes into account everything to do with the preparation and rehearsal period and demands that every member of your company works together to achieve the best possible results. This section carries a possible total of 15 marks.
- Final performance/designs: this sets out the criteria that will be applied to the final performance and designs presented for assessment. This section carries a possible total of 30 marks.
- Evaluation of own work: this allows you to review and assess the effectiveness of your contribution to the overall effectiveness of the performance. This section carries a possible total of 15 marks.

The equal marks for 'skills development and professional conduct' and for 'evaluation of own work' emphasise the importance of these areas. You should give them appropriate consideration. The marks for these two areas will be decided by your teacher before the final performance and offered for moderation on the moderation day.

The mark for 'final performance/designs' will be given by your teacher and moderated by the visiting moderator appointed by AQA.

Activity

2 Record your progress

As you work through the research and rehearsal period, all members of the company must keep a detailed record of what happens. You should focus on how the ideas develop and how you and your fellow company members employ the skills, in rehearsal, that you have developed during the course. These notes will be needed when you evaluate your work.

Some points to remember:

- your research should include looking at the work of others
- you should carry out a skills audit before starting the rehearsal period
- you will need to write observations of the work of others in the company and make copies available with the evaluations
- you must refer to the brief throughout the process and call regular meetings to ensure deadlines are met
- you must ensure that rehearsals are being carried out effectively
- designers, technicians and production team must be organised and draw up clear work schedules
- you will need to have your target audience in mind throughout the planning and rehearsal period
- once you have allocated roles and responsibilities keep each other informed of any problems that may arise.

The list above is a guide only and you should be prepared to add to it if appropriate.

Chapter 4 Final showcase performance

> ### Activity
> ### 3 Evaluation
> Read through the notes, observations and research that you have collected and start to select material to be included in the final evaluation. Follow the suggestions in chapter 1 to help you bring together all the elements of the evaluation.
>
> Your final evaluation must include details of your contribution to planning, preparation and skills development. You must also include **three** observations of your working practices by people with whom you have worked.
>
> You will need to present the evaluation on one side of A2, two sides of A3 or four sides of A4 paper.

Prepare your performance

Once you have taken time to read the showcase brief and made any notes to help understanding what is required you are ready to follow the 'seven steps to success' that will take you through the rehearsal process and on to the final performance.

Plan your time carefully and you will achieve the best possible results. Once you reach the final stages of the rehearsal period and are ready for your dress and technical rehearsals you should also consider writing your evaluation.

Moderation day

Having completed the rehearsal and preparation period you will be ready for the final performance and moderation.

Your teacher will have observed you throughout the rehearsal period and will have allocated you a mark for skills' development and professional conduct. Your evaluations will also have been marked and will be ready for the visiting moderator to read.

The visiting moderator will be introduced to you and your company and make you feel at ease and you must accept that from your point of view the moderator is just another member of the audience.

Remember your teacher will be marking your performance using the assessment criteria that you were issued with in the original brief. At the end of the performance, your teacher will record your marks and the moderation will be over.

The important thing to remember is to enjoy the experience and work with confidence and as a member of the company.

B *Your teacher will have observed you through the rehearsal period*

UNIT THREE and UNIT FOUR

GCSE Performing Arts is offered as a single GCSE and a double award. The rest of this book concentrates on Units 3 and 4, which you must complete in addition to Units 1 and 2 for the double award. Units 1 and 2 were covered previously in this book.

UNIT THREE Working to a Commission

Internally assessed and externally moderated.

Marked out of 70 (30% of the total marks for the double award GCSE)

Students build on the experience skills development and professional conduct established in Unit 1 through practical involvement.

Practice commission 1
Street life

Practice commission 2
Musical theatre

Practice commission 3
Carnival!

UNIT FOUR Final Performance/Designs for the Chosen Commission

Internally assessed and externally moderated.

Marked out of 60 (20% of the total marks for the double award GCSE)

Students work as a production company to put on a performance in response to a showcase brief

Exam period 1 February – 31 May

Showcase performance

UNIT THREE and UNIT FOUR 51

In Unit 3, you develop further your skills based on the work for Units 1 and 2. You will increase your knowledge through working on the practice commissions. You will create a second portfolio that reflects the work you do.

You should also begin to prepare a CV based on the range of work developed in Units 1 and 2. You will add to your CV as you improve your skills in Units 3 and 4. You will also research the working practices of professional performers. Your portfolio must show evidence that you have used ideas from professionals.

In Unit 4, the work you do is based on the work carried out in Unit 3. Unit 4 gives you the chance to demonstrate what you have learned about working as part of a team and how to present your personal skills. You work with the rest of your performing arts group to produce a performance to meet a commission set by AQA. You should include the work you do for the final commission in the portfolio you compile for Unit 3.

In both Units 3 and 4, you follow a process that includes the seven steps to success.

Seven Steps to Success

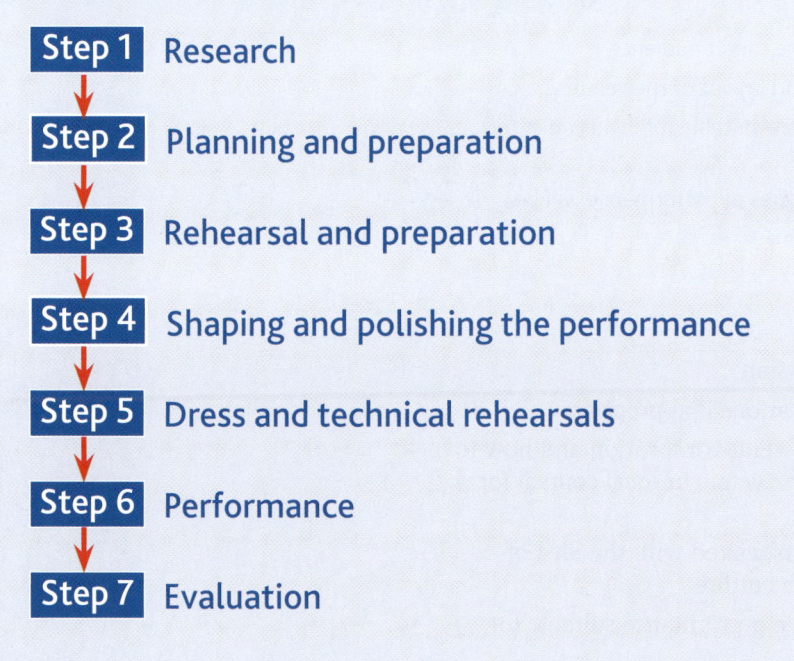

- Step 1 Research
- Step 2 Planning and preparation
- Step 3 Rehearsal and preparation
- Step 4 Shaping and polishing the performance
- Step 5 Dress and technical rehearsals
- Step 6 Performance
- Step 7 Evaluation

UNIT THREE: Working to a commission

Practice commission 1

5 Street life

Read the practice commission below very carefully and consider each of the bullet points. Your teacher will take on the role of **commissioner**.

Street life

As part of a nationwide celebration of youth culture your local education authority is organising a performance event to coincide with similar events throughout the country.

- The theme is '**street life**'.
- The target audience is the local community.
- The objective is to inform through performance.
- The constraints are:
  - You will research appropriate local venues and outdoor locations.
  - Choose one of the venues or outdoor locations for your performance.
  - You will be expected to put on **three** performances in the chosen venue.
  - You will put on a matinee performance at 2pm and an evening performance at 7pm on the first day and the third performance at 7pm the following evening. You must take into consideration time for get-in and get-out.

Your company must present **two performance proposals** for consideration by the commissioner. The proposals should include the following:

- Evidence of research into the needs of the target audience.
- Evidence of research into the facilities and layout of the venues.
- Evidence of the range of materials that are suitable for inclusion in the performance.
- An indication as to how the styles and types of performance will be suitable for the commission.

Key terms

Commissioner: the person or group that asks you to take part in the performance event and sets the constraints for the performance.

Performance proposals: written documents that set out your ideas for the performance. Each proposal should include a brief description of the ideas to be included in the performance and any special technical requirements.

It is expected that you will:

- create a performance to fit the commission
- research suitable venues or outside locations if appropriate
- explore the availability of your chosen venue or location and how to gain the necessary permissions from the venue or local council for outside locations
- explore the range of performing arts associated with the idea of 'street life' and the celebration of youth culture
- choose appropriate art forms to create a performance suitable for your target audience
- understand the need for effective planning and management of all aspects of the performance process
- understand the importance of health and safety issues.

How to get started

It is important to understand that the demands of this part of the course are slightly different from those of Unit 1 and Unit 2. The commission attempts to put you into a situation where you can work and develop your skills to the highest possible standard. It also gives you the opportunity to reflect on industry practices where professional companies must submit two proposals to the commissioner for consideration. Your teacher will act as commissioner and will supervise the process from beginning to end, offering advice and writing observations on your work.

As you start to work on the practice commissions you must also start to think about preparing a curriculum vitae (CV) that reflects your experiences and the skills that you have learned. You will be expected to build your CV as you progress.

A very important part of Unit 3 is the contextual understanding of work-related aspects. In other words, you will be expected to research the work and practices of people working in your chosen skill area and adopt a work-related approach to your own work.

Once you have read the commission and understood what is required, your production company will plan the two performance proposals. However before anything can go ahead, all the company members will need to carry out a personal skills audit. Choose the performing arts disciplines to be included and identify any disciplines that you want to learn.

AQA Examiner's tip

You should look carefully at the skills audits that you carried out for Unit 1 and Unit 2 and use them as the starting point for this exercise.

Remember

You need to offer your best possible skills if you are to achieve the best results. Every member of the company should have the opportunity to show their strengths.

A *There are a wide variety of possibilities for this theme*

Activity

1 Production meeting

Call a production company meeting and consider the spider-gram of skills in diagram **B**. It is worth considering all 17 performing arts disciplines when listing the areas that you would like to explore. Consider the skills of your company when making your lists.

You will need to carry out some wider research with this theme before making your final choices. You will need to consider the different styles of performance you might include, for example break dancing rather than more conventional forms of dance.

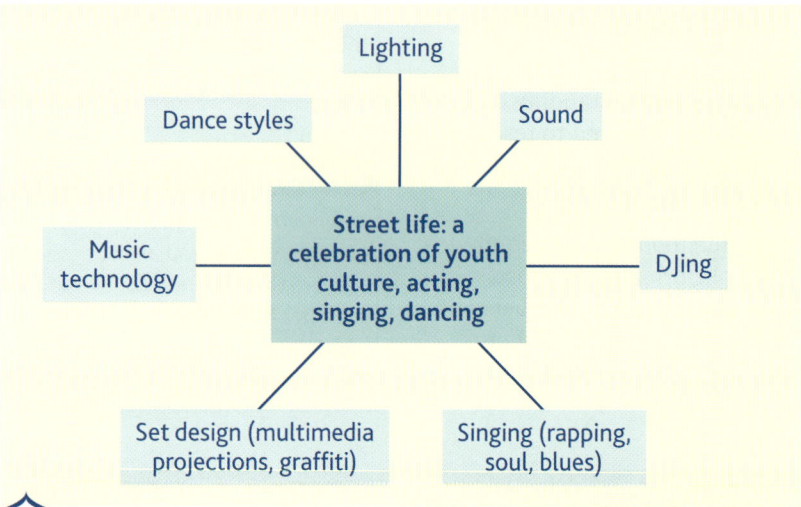

```
                    Lighting
    Dance styles              Sound

                Street life: a
  Music        celebration of youth      DJing
  technology   culture, acting,
               singing, dancing

   Set design (multimedia    Singing (rapping,
   projections, graffiti)    soul, blues)
```

B Some of the performing arts disciplines you could use to fulfil this commission

C You must make best use of your strengths

Chapter 5 Street life 55

Step 1 Research

Having formed your production company and identified the areas you would like to explore further you can start to research the theme in detail. The need for detailed research cannot be stressed enough because you will need to write the proposals based on your findings.

D *Your research must be thorough*

Key terms

Screever: a licensed artist who draws with chalks on pavements and public areas. The pictures are usually of famous paintings, portraits of personalities or optical illusions. Screevers often draw onto canvas and carry their work away at the end of the day.

Buskers: musicians who play under license in public places such as shopping centres and tube stations.

Banksy: an artist famous for the high quality of his graffiti art. His work often reflects images from life, is highly regarded and is protected by local authorities against damage. Others imitate his work. See picture **E** for an example of his work.

Activity

2 Research the theme

In small groups or as individuals, choose one of the following areas to research:

- street artists (**screevers**)
- **buskers**
- mime artists
- street dance (break dancing)
- DJing
- street performers (jugglers, acrobats)
- graffiti artists (**Banksy**)
- popular music/songs with appropriate lyrics reflecting street life and youth culture
- rapping, steel bands, blues and soul music
- street sports that might form the basis of movement (roller-blading, skateboarding, free running)
- street festivals and celebrations (Chinese New Year)
- improvised or scripted monologues/duologues about aspects of street life
- fashion and costume worn by different youth groups.

Prepare a short PowerPoint presentation on 'street life' based on your research and present it to your fellow company members and the commissioner.

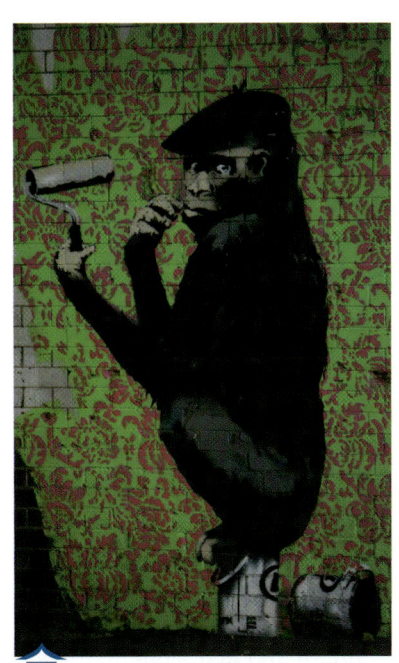

E *Work by stencil graffiti artist Bansky*

F 3D artist Kurt Wenner

Extension activity

1 Visit your local town centre and observe local street artists and performers. Take some photographs and include them in your portfolio. Or, if there are no such activities in your area, use the internet, but remember to annotate them. Before you take your photographs you may well need to ask permission of the artist or performer. List the skills that you have observed and discuss your findings with other company members.

Display your photographs and research materials so that all members of your company can refer to them in your planning meetings. Discuss your research and decide which aspects of 'street life' will form the basis of your proposals and what skills you are going to include in your proposed performances. Actors will need to think about scripting ideas; dancers about creating suitable choreography in a range of dance styles; singers will choose appropriate songs; and the technical team will consider the need for set, lighting, sound, stage management, front of house and marketing.

Chapter 5 Street life 57

Extension activity

2   Watch extracts from the film *West Side Story* and look at how music, dance and drama mix to create not only an exciting story but an energetic look at street life in America in the 1960s. If you have the opportunity to visit a live performance think about the way in which the performers need to have acting, singing and dance skills.

West Side Story was based on Shakespeare's *Romeo and Juliet* and is a good example of how an established and well-known love story can be used to create an effective piece of modern theatre and film history.

Can you think of other stage shows or films that deal with similar themes or explore some of the activities that you have researched? Watching other people's performances can be a useful inspiration for your own work. Make notes and add them to your portfolio.

G   *Scenes from* West Side Story, *1961*

Step 2 Planning and preparation

The commission is clearly open to interpretation and this is why you are asked to prepare **two proposals** for consideration. Your teacher, as the commissioner, will choose the one that best suits the theme and allows each company to explore their chosen skills to the highest level possible. In planning your proposals it is important to make sure that your ideas are clear and detailed.

Activity

3 Presenting the proposals

In small groups or as an individual prepare two proposals for consideration. Discuss the proposals in groups and decide on the final two to present to the commissioner. All of the proposals should be kept in your portfolios for future reference.

What to include in the proposal:

- name of the production company
- list of company members and their skills, strengths and weaknesses
- title or theme of the work to be presented
- target audience
- details of the proposed performance venue; this may well include diagrams and plans of the venue
- times and dates
- proposed running time of the performance
- the proposed rehearsal schedule
- an outline of the content of the proposed performance
- the art forms to be included
- any technical requirements, such as lighting or sound
- details of set and costumes
- a list of physical resources that will be needed, for example rehearsal space, equipment such as musical instruments, props
- a suggested budget if appropriate.

> **AQA Examiner's tip**
> It is important to make your proposals as detailed as possible because these will form the basis of all the work that follows.

> **Remember**
> All the proposals are important and you might decide to use ideas from more than one as you select what to finally present to the commissioner. Everyone in the company should be happy with the final two proposals. Once your teacher, as commissioner, chooses your final proposal it will be difficult to change your minds without lengthy negotiations, unless you realise something has gone seriously wrong.

As soon as you have all the proposals you will need to select the two to be put forward. You will need to be realistic in your choices and may need to adapt the proposals slightly to meet the needs of the company.

Activity

4 Company meeting

Once the commissioner has selected the proposal you will need to call a company meeting to consider the next steps in the preparation of the final performance.

- Draw up an action plan
- Allocate roles and responsibilities. You will have indicated some of these in your proposal.
- Arrange rehearsal times and spaces.
- Take note of any suggestions made by the commissioner.

> **Hint**
> Call meetings at regular intervals and review your action plans. Place all your action plans in your portfolio alongside all your research and proposals.

Chapter 5   Street life   59

Step 3   Rehearsal

Be very clear about what you have to do to meet the demands of the commission and keep to the deadline. Look back at your accepted proposal and make sure that all company members understand their individual roles and responsibilities.

This part of the process should take approximately 30 hours depending on the size of your company and your final performance should be between 10 and 30 minutes long. If your group is small then you will need to work towards 10 minutes and if larger then you are more likely to work towards the 30 minutes suggested. Your teacher will advise you on this if you are not sure.

Activity

5   Develop the final 'script' or 'running order'

As you rehearse you will need to develop the final 'script' or running order. Record all the details of:

- improvised scenes and text that may be fixed
- choreography and dance styles
- musical items
- specialist acts, for example break or street dancing, Capoeira displays, DJ-ing, juggling, acrobatic acts.

AQA Examiner's tip

You are already aware of the time constraints from working through the practice briefs in chapter 1 and presenting your final performance for Unit 2. However it is easy to forget when you are creating a new work.

Once you have decided on the content of the final performance it is always a good idea to 'run' the pieces and time them. It is better to have a clear idea of running times early in the process rather than at the end when cutting causes extra problems.

AQA Examiner's tip

Observing each other in rehearsal is important as this forms part of the evaluation process. You should be prepared to discuss what you see in a positive way but equally be prepared to take criticism and act upon it.

H Cast in rehearsals, Orange Tree Theatre, Richmond

Remember

If you need to remind yourself about 'the Book' turn to pages 22–23 in chapter 1.

The rehearsal process is not new to you and provided that you have worked through the course so far you will be aware of the importance of watching each other in rehearsal. If there is no one to take the role of stage manager, you will also have realised the need to create 'the Book'.

Be aware of the health-and-safety requirements of your specific style of performance. The more active and energetic the performance the more careful you should be.

> **Activity**
>
> **6 Risk assessment**
>
> All members of the company should carry out risk assessments on aspects of
> - the performance
> - the rehearsal space
> - the chosen performance space.
>
> Make recommendations to ensure that all aspects of the rehearsal and performance spaces are safe. You should make notes of any changes in the rehearsal process that you make as a result of the risk assessments and say why.

The technical members of the company should be particularly aware of health and safety as they are working with potentially dangerous equipment. If there is any doubt about the safety of lighting or sound equipment ask your teacher first before using it. Always follow the instructions provided and never overload the system.

If you are building a set, secure all pieces of scenery with ropes, braces and weights. Find out the local fire regulations as these often give advice about fireproofing pieces of scenery and costumes.

The house management team will be responsible for keeping exits and entrances to the performance space clear and fixing seating for the audience. This is especially important if your final performance is to take place in a different venue from the rehearsal space or in an outside space.

As in previous rehearsal periods, all members of the company should be prepared to help wherever necessary and must remember to record the process in detail. You should call regular production meetings and keep records of all the minutes and action plans in your portfolio. It is very important to remember that the portfolio for Unit 3 should reflect the working process that you have gone through in order to reach the final performance of your commission proposal.

By this stage in the course you should have developed an excellent sense of working as a team and helping each other. The more trust you have with each other as performers the stronger the company and more effective the final performance.

During the final stages of rehearsal it is even more important to develop a routine that includes physical and vocal warm ups for the performers.

Throughout the rehearsal period it is also expected that you will develop your understanding of other performers, designers and technicians and how they communicate their ideas to the audience. When you visit the theatre or watch performances on television and film you should start to identify people who impress you and consider the ways in which they are effective. You might be impressed with their characterisation or the way in which they are able to work with an audience.

> **Activity**
>
> **7 Assess venue safety**
>
> All members of the company should consider the need for safety at the venue chosen for the performance and draw a plan of the auditorium and performance space, clearly showing:
> - exits and entrances
> - fire points
> - fire extinguishers
> - distances between aisles and the performance area.

> **Remember**
>
> Remind yourself about warm-ups. Look at chapter 1.

Combine your skills to create a great overall performance

A dancer will be able to impress with accurate footwork and command of the space, a lighting designer with an atmospheric use of colour that enhances the overall performance.

It is well worth taking time to think about the contribution made to the performing arts by other performers, technicians, designers and members of the administrative and marketing teams and try to answer the question 'Why are they effective and is there anything that I can learn from them?' You shouldn't just consider the famous but also those working at the local repertory theatre or the small-scale touring company that visits your school. You might also have the opportunity to attend workshops run by a professional working in the performing arts, as these can be an invaluable source of information and knowledge and link directly with the work-related aspects of the course.

Extension activity

3 Your teacher may be able to arrange a backstage tour at a local theatre where you would be able to find out more about the work that happens behind the scenes. This is always a useful way to understand job roles and responsibilities. It also gives you some idea of what might be expected of you not only in rehearsal but also in performance.

AQA Examiner's tip

The course expects you to explore the work of others in a work-related context. You should develop your understanding of this aspect of your work and start to use it to develop your own performances. Make sure that you record any information that you find and highlight it in your portfolio.

You should review your progress and check that you have met the demands of the original commission and, very importantly, that your proposal still meets the demands of the commission. As you approach the end of your rehearsal period, you should have all the elements of the performance ready for the next stage including any technical requirements, props, costumes and set. You should also have all specialist equipment available, **cue sheets**, schedules and action plans in place. It is also important to consider the administrative aspect of the performance, such as front of house.

J Props and technical equipment must be prepared

The course also requires you to provide two **observations** of the work that you and the other members of your production company have taken part in during the rehearsal period. These observations will need to be included in the portfolio. Your teacher will provide one of the observations and you will need to provide one for the other members of your company.

Key terms

Cue sheet: a list of actors' lines, musical effect, set or choreography and the technical task to be carried out when the line is spoken or an action completed.

Observation: a short written report by a teacher or a member of your performing arts group commenting on your work.

Activity

8 Peer observations

Observations of other members of the company are important and must be included in your portfolio.
- You will need to include as much detail as possible.
- Keep notes about the rehearsals and how the company develops.
- Make sure that you identify the strengths rather than the weaknesses of your company members.

You might find it easier to build up your observation over the rehearsal period rather than leaving it to the last minute.

Step 4 Shaping and polishing the performance

Once you have reached this stage in the process you need to 'run' the performance and make sure that all company members fully understand what they have to do. This is your opportunity to fine tune the performance. You will no doubt find problems with running times or need to adjust the performance space to ease the flow of the performance. You may need to carry out minor adjustments to the set or costumes and make changes to the technical requirements.

- As performers, this is the time to work on refining the different skills that you have employed and make any final adjustments to your work.
- As a designer, this is an important step in the process because it is the time that all your hard work begins to come together. You will be able to assess if the set works or the costumes fit.
- As a technician, you have the opportunity to fine tune the lights and sound, checking the health-and-safety aspects of the performance space and making clear copies of your cue sheets.
- As a member of the administration and marketing teams you should have the posters ready and seating plans prepared.

> **Remember**
> Refresh your memory of the process by looking back at the work that you did earlier in the course. You might find it useful to look at pages 26–27 in chapter 1.

K *All aspects of your performance should be planned out, even elements you want to seem casual to an audience*

Step 5 Dress and technical rehearsals

It is well worth taking time to review the process you have taken part in so far before going into the dress and technical rehearsals. Call a meeting of the production company and make sure that everyone is aware of what is needed.

Activity

9 Production company meeting

Refresh your memory by looking back to the activity in chapter 1 page 22. It is well worth following the check list that is given. Think back to the last time that you performed and make a list of things that you feel need to be improved to make sure the performance runs smoothly.

L Working hard on your skills together is very important

The success of the final performance will depend on teamwork and that means every member of your production company working together to achieve the best possible results. If there is a weak link it will show. It is therefore important to be able to help and assist your fellow team members to prepare for this vital stage in the process.

Remember
You cannot blame others for things that go wrong if you are aware of the problem and haven't tried to solve it.

Step 6 The performance

You have managed to get through the rehearsal process, everything is in place, roles and responsibilities are clear, the time for the final performance has arrived.

As you prepare to perform you need to focus and use all the skills that you have rehearsed effectively but also be aware of what is about to take place. You will have to be flexible and respond to things that may not have happened in rehearsal. The important thing is that you and your fellow company members are confident and well rehearsed; discipline in performance is essential.

After the performance you will need to make sure that you have carried out all the tasks associated with clearing the performance space such as checking off props and costumes, striking the set and de-rigging technical equipment. All members of the company should be prepared to lend a hand at this point in order to bring the performance to a clear and successful end.

Designers will need to check that all their artefacts are safe and photographs of sets and costumes are safely stored in portfolios.

Activity

10 Focus on roles and responsibilities

Consider the roles and responsibilities of the company for the chosen performance. Make a list of the roles and responsibilities giving a brief description of each one outlining what will be needed for the performance.

You must include all the performing arts disciplines that you have included in your commission. Take a look at diagram **B**, page 8.

AQA Examiner's tip

Your teacher will be assessing you using the assessment grid in the specification. Your teacher has also acted as the commissioner and will know whether or not you have kept to the accepted proposal.

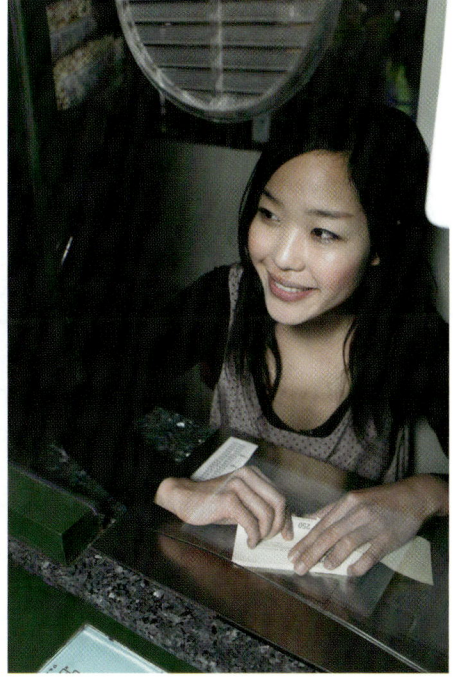

You must consider all aspects of the performance and its organisation

Step 7 Evaluation

The importance of the evaluation cannot be stressed enough. Just as with the portfolio for Unit 1 and the performance that you gave in Unit 2 you need to consider your part in the process and that of the other members of your company. Write your evaluations following the stages set out in chapter 1, pages 29–30 and keep the finished pieces in your portfolio.

The main areas to consider are:

- evaluation of your own work
- evaluation of planning and research
- evaluation of practical activities
- knowledge and contextual understanding of work-related aspects
- evaluation of your own and others' work.

The activity that follows gives you a checklist of things to include in the final evaluation, read it carefully and make sure that you have all the information needed.

The checklist in the activity below is only a guide. You might think of other things that you want to include. The important thing is that you are able to look positively on the experience and use it to develop your skills when you work on your next commission.

Activity

11 Evaluation

As you begin to bring together all the information, notes, observations and research for the evaluation you should consider the following points:

- Did you prepare thoroughly for the rehearsal period?
- Were you prepared for the dress and technical runs of the performance?
- Did you fully understand the roles and responsibilities that were allocated to you?
- Did you understand the need for 'professional' behaviour throughout the process?
- Were you aware of the constraints on the performance space or venue and were you able to adapt to them?
- Were you aware of the health and safety issues surrounding the rehearsals and performances?
- Were you able to take direction and work effectively between rehearsals?
- Did you take responsibility for your personal belongings at all times?
- Did you warm up appropriately?
- If you were part of the technical team did you have all the necessary cue sheets ready?
- If you were a designer did you have all the necessary plans, costumes and props ready?
- If you were the stage manager did you have 'the Book' and all the cue sheets ready?
- If you were responsible for organising the front of house did you plan and look after the audience appropriately?
- If you were responsible for the marketing, how effective was your publicity campaign?
- Did you respond to instructions effectively?
- Did you maintain discipline throughout the performance?
- Were you able to sustain the performance?
- Did you work well as a member of the team?

As you approach your next commission, whether you are a performer, designer, technician or part of the stage-management crew or the front of house and marketing team, you need to have confidence in your chosen skill or skills. You now need to focus on what you do really well because these skills will probably be the ones that you will use in the final commission performance. If you have any doubts you should discuss them with your teacher who has been observing you throughout the process and will be able to give you advice. Of course you will also have all the observations and notes in your portfolio from various stages in the rehearsal process, these are an important resource. Don't forget to use them to improve your skills even further.

Activity

12 Review the skills audit

Once you have completed the evaluation, look back over the skills audit that you made at the start of the process and review your progress. It is very important that you identify things to work on at this point because you need to understand your strengths and weaknesses before moving on to the next commission. For example, you might decide that you need to improve the quality of your breathing in order to sing the more demanding aspects of a song or make sense of a speech or work on your ability to lift your partner higher in the dance. If you are responsible for administration and marketing, you might need to work on publicity.

N Enjoy your success

Practice commission 2

6 Musical theatre

You must read the commission below very carefully and consider all of the bullet points.

Musical theatre

Your company has been invited to produce and perform the school's annual musical theatre production.

- The theme is open to discussion.
- The target audience is the local community.
- The objective is entertainment.
- The constraints are:
  - you will perform in your school hall/theatre
  - you will be expected to put on three consecutive performances
  - you have a budget of £3000.

Your company must present **two** performance proposals for consideration by the commissioner. The proposals should include the following:

- evidence of research into the needs of the target audience
- evidence of research into the range of suitable musicals available
- evidence of how the budget will be spent including performance rights
- an indication as to how the styles and types of performances will be suitable for the commission.

A *Billboards advertising theatre musicals*

It is expected that you will:

- produce a performance that will fit in with the **commission**
- research **musical theatre** and its history
- choose an appropriate musical for performance at your school
- understand the need for effective planning and management of all aspects of the performance process
- research and show understanding of performing rights and licences
- understand the importance of health and safety issues.

> **Key terms**
>
> **Commission**: a special assignment that is given to a person or a group.
>
> **Musical theatre**: an art form whose action and dialogue is interspersed with singing and dancing.

How to get started

Refer to the information given to you in chapter 5, 'Street life'. Make sure that you reassess your skill levels.

B Some of the performing arts disciplines you could use to fulfil this commission

C Mamma Mia, a musical based on the songs of pop group ABBA. Look up what is meant by 'juke-box musical'

Activity

1 Production meeting

As a production company, get together to hold your first meeting. During the meeting remember to allocated roles. This sets professional conduct from the start and shows organisation.

Produce an action plan of how your time is going to be spent up to the presentation of proposals to the commissioner. Make sure that you divide the research between the different members of your company and have regular meetings to report back to each other.

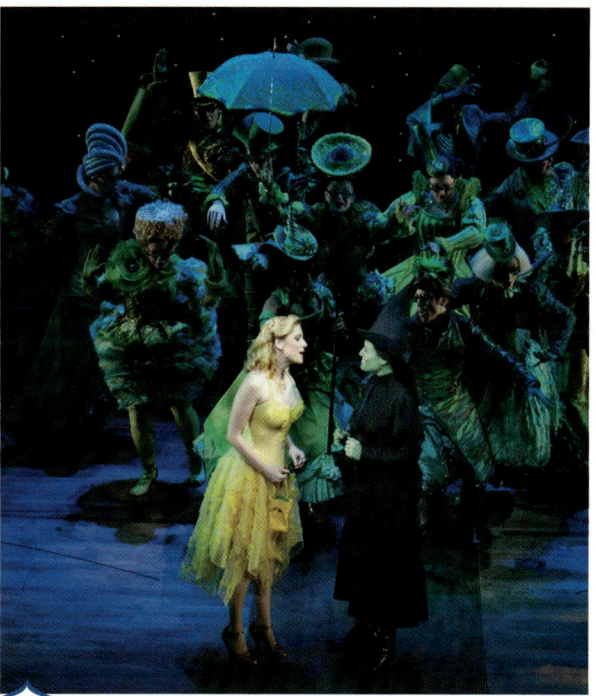

D Wicked, a musical based on a novel

Step 1 Research

The commission clearly states that you are to organise the annual school musical. As well as researching the topic, you must also show research into the history of musicals, and into the target audience. You must also stick to your budget of £3000 and observe all health and safety regulations.

Here are some suggestions for topics for your research:

- What is musical theatre?
- How and when did musical theatre start?
- **Book musical.**
- Broadway musicals.
- Famous composers, for example Rodgers and Hammerstein, Andrew Lloyd Webber.
- Famous musical theatre performers, for example Ruthie Henshall, Lea Salonga, Michael Ball, Colm Wilkinson.
- Themes and storylines.
- How musical theatre has evolved.
- Target audience.
- Performance rights.

Did you know

In *The Phantom of the Opera*, the dazzling replica of the Paris Opera House chandelier is made up of 6000 beads, is 3m wide and weighs 500 kg.

E *The chandelier from* The Phantom of the Opera

F *Performers in* The Lion King *musical*

Key terms

Book musical: a form very dependent on plot and character that integrates the script with the musical themes; popular in the mid-20th century.

Hint

You may wish to present scenes from a selection of different musicals to make up your final commission performance.

AQA Examiner's tip

Make sure you find out from the commissioner why he/she selected the proposal you are to continue with and write it in your portfolio.

Step 2 Planning and preparation

The next stage is to hold a production meeting and collate all the research that people have gathered. It is usually a good idea to have a 'chairperson' to lead the meeting and a 'secretary' to take notes of what is said and decided. Taking into consideration the skills that are on offer from your group and the target audience you now need to list all the findings and ideas you have taken from your research.

It is important to remember that everyone is working together as a team and that everyone should be developing ideas for inclusion in the final performance. Refer back to the commission to make sure that you are still meeting the requirements.

You should be developing the two proposals that you will be presenting to the commissioner. Don't worry if you have too many ideas – it is always better to have too much than not enough and the commissioner can suggest ways forward in the feedback you are given afterwards.

Each proposal should show detailed research and a clear understanding of how your company intends the performance to be. Your proposals should include all the performing arts disciplines that your company is providing and where possible, illustrations should be presented.

The activity box below gives you an idea of what should be included in a proposal.

> **Remember**
> All minutes from meetings can be copied for everyone's portfolios, provided credit is given to the person who wrote them.

> **AQA Examiner's tip**
> Meetings and minutes show that you have acted professionally and can therefore count towards marks for 'Contextual understanding of work-related aspects'.

Activity

2 The proposal

Make sure you include the following information:
- the outline for the finished performance and the art forms to be used
- the roles and responsibilities of the members of your production company
- the musical you have chosen and why you have chosen it
- the excerpts of the musical you will perform
- rehearsal space required
- equipment required
- target audience information
- how the proposal meets the objective.

> **AQA Examiner's tip**
> Be professional! Think of the task of presenting your proposals as an interview for a job. Take the opportunity to dress smartly to create a good impression.

Each member of your company should take responsibility for a different part of the research and you can divide the presentation of your proposals between the different members of your company.

Proposals can be presented in all sorts of ways – for example, PowerPoint, hand outs or flip charts – but remember the more detail you include the more it will help you later on.

Once you have presented the two proposals, each member of the production company must include a copy of them in their portfolios. It is always a good idea to annotate them to give an explanation of what was said during the presentation.

> **Remember**
> The commission is asking you to produce the school musical, which you will probably perform in full. You only need to perform extracts.

Contextual understanding of work-related aspects

This is a vital part of the portfolio for the commission and is different from the work-related activities you did in Unit 1. Read on for ways of completing this section.

> **Remember**
> For this unit you must clearly be able to show how professionals work and demonstrate how you have experimented with their ideas and how you have been influenced by their work.

> *All the best performers bring to their role something more, something different than what the author put on paper. That's what makes theatre live. That's why it persists.*
>
> Stephen Sondheim

G *Writer of musicals, Stephen Sondheim*

As well as providing a case study for how your performance has been influenced by professional ideas, you must also continue to research the roles and responsibilities within the industry but in more detail than for Unit 1. Concentrate on the role that you are taking in the production company. Find some professionals – use the internet to contact them. Ask them questions about their jobs but don't get too personal! There is also a useful careers website given in the links box that has case studies with certain jobs. If you have any visiting actors in school, don't miss the opportunity to ask them about their jobs.

You also need to make sure that you have some warm-up techniques ready to use with your company before every rehearsal.

H *Think carefully about all aspects of the performance*

Chapter 6 Musical theatre 73

I *Rex Harrison and Audrey Hepburn in* My Fair Lady

J *Johnathan Pryce as Henry Higgings in* My Fair Lady

Activity

3 Performer research

Imagine that you are a performer for your production company and you will be performing 'I've grown accustomed to her face' from *My Fair Lady*. Look at a performance of the song – for example, Jonathan Pryce's performance in *Hey Mr Producer*. Write a review of his performance:

- What did you like about it?
- What didn't you like about it?
- Was it sung, spoken or both?
- What blocking did he do?
- What mannerisms did he give to the character?
- What ideas could you use in your performance and how would they make your performance better?

You could then follow this up by comparing the Jonathan Pryce performance with another performance, such as Rex Harrison playing Henry Higgins in the film version of *My Fair Lady*.

Step 3 Rehearsal and preparation

Having presented your proposals and had one chosen by the commissioner, it is now time to think about the rehearsal process aiming to an end result in the final performance.

Activity

4 Production meeting

Call a production meeting so that everyone can remind themselves of the chosen commission and their roles and begin to work on a time frame for rehearsals.

- How much time do you have for rehearsal? The specification suggests 30 hours but this is going to be flexible depending on the size of your company and the time allocated by your teacher.
- Divide your piece into sections (scenes) for rehearsal – can two scenes be rehearsed at the same time?
- Make sure that everybody has something to do for each rehearsal.
- When do you need costumes and set to be ready?
- Leave time at the end of your rehearsal schedule for at least two technical and dress rehearsals. Make time for production meetings throughout the rehearsal process.
- Try to get an audience for the dress rehearsal so that you can be given valuable feedback.

Remember

Keep a record of every rehearsal but make sure that it is detailed so it can be valuable evidence in your portfolio.

- What was achieved?
- What was not achieved?
- What skills did you learn/develop?
- Who worked well/didn't work well?
- Your next steps.
- The group's next steps.

AQA Examiner's tip

Ask someone to take photographs of you during rehearsals – especially if you are demonstrating a skill – then make sure you annotate it so it can go into your portfolio.

Teamwork is vital especially during the rehearsal period. Even though you are being marked as an individual you are still performing as and working together as a company.

K *Planning will help make the most of your rehearsals*

Step 4 Shaping and polishing the performance

It is important that you start to put different parts of the performances together as soon as possible during the rehearsal process and mix them with the technical areas. As before, make sure that everybody is involved in rehearsals and if there are people who aren't busy, get them to watch your rehearsal so they can add constructive comments.

Begin to use any props, set and costumes when they are ready so that you are used to performing with them. Refer back to the previous chapters to remind yourself of more detail for shaping and polishing the performance.

> 66 I tend to arrive in the rehearsal process with very strongly developed ideas about what I want to do. But I don't like those ideas to be things that are not subject to change, or subject to development, or subject to challenge. 99
>
> Trevor Nunn

Actor, Trevor Nunn

Remember
- Work together as a company.
- Stick to the agreed rehearsal schedule.
- Be aware of all of the different parts of the production that go together to make the final product.
- Be professional at all times.
- Keep a record of your work.
- Work to the best of your ability.

Step 5 Technical and dress rehearsals

At this point you need to make sure that you are referring back to Street life, chapter 5 on page 64 to remind yourself what the technical and dress rehearsals require. Remember to get an audience together so you can receive valuable feedback and, if possible, record your rehearsal on video so you can see what is working and what isn't.

Remember
Make sure that before all rehearsals you warm up both physically and vocally.

Step 6 The performance

It's opening night! Your front-of-house team has been busy selling tickets to your audience and you have a packed house. You must remember that this performance is also for your GCSE Unit 4 performance. As well as working as a member of a team, you need to perform your best as an individual.

It is important for actors, singers and performers to warm their muscles before a show. If they go on stage "cold" it could lead to strain and physical injury. Research warm-up exercises and practise with your peers to discover which ones work best.

AQA Examiner's tip
Take lots of photographs of your musical in performance and put them in your portfolio with relevant comments. It is always easier to write about something if you can see it.

Step 7 Evaluation

The evaluation process is very important. You will have been evaluating your progress throughout this chapter but you must now thoroughly evaluate the whole process from beginning to end as well as the final performance. Remember to write about other people as well as yourself and evaluate your skills since you started this chapter. Refer to chapter 5, pages 66–67 for more detail on what to include in your evaluation.

links
www.musicals101.com
www.josef-weinberger.co.uk
www.nodanw.co.uk
www.musicals.net

Practice commission 3

7 Carnival!

Culture

Your local council is organising a week of events that celebrates the cultural diversity of different communities that live in your area. The final performance will be a carnival based on the culture of a country, or countries, of your choice.

- The theme is '**culture**'.
- The target audience is the local community.
- The objective is education and celebration through entertainment.
- The constraints are:
  - you will research appropriate performance spaces and choose one for your performance
  - you will be expected to put on **two** performances in the chosen space
  - you will put on a matinee performance at 2.00pm and an evening performance at 7.00pm.

Your company must present **two** performance proposals for consideration by the commissioner.

The proposals should include the following:

- evidence of research into the needs of the target audience
- evidence of research into the facilities and performance areas available to you
- evidence of the range of materials that are suitable for inclusion in the performance
- an indication of how the styles and types of performances will be suitable for the commission.

> **Remember**
> Refresh your memory of the key terms with the Glossary on pages 90–91.

> *Carnival arts open the door to a world of self-expression and exploration; a unique place where we can seek out our roots and develop new forums for uniting the planet's bountiful cultures. A place for discovering what we all have in common, and celebrating what makes us different. The power and creativity that underlies these art forms can transform lives.*

As in the previous practice commissions, you must read the commission very carefully and consider all of the bullet points.

Chapter 6 Carnival! 77

A *Carnivals have a special place in some communities*

It is expected that you will:

- create a performance that will fit in with the commission
- research suitable performance spaces, platforms
- explore the range of performing arts associated with the ideas of culture and carnival
- choose appropriate art forms to create a performance suitable for your target audience
- understand the need for effective planning and management of all aspects of the performance process
- understand the importance of health-and-safety issues.

B *Carnival floats are meant to make an impact*

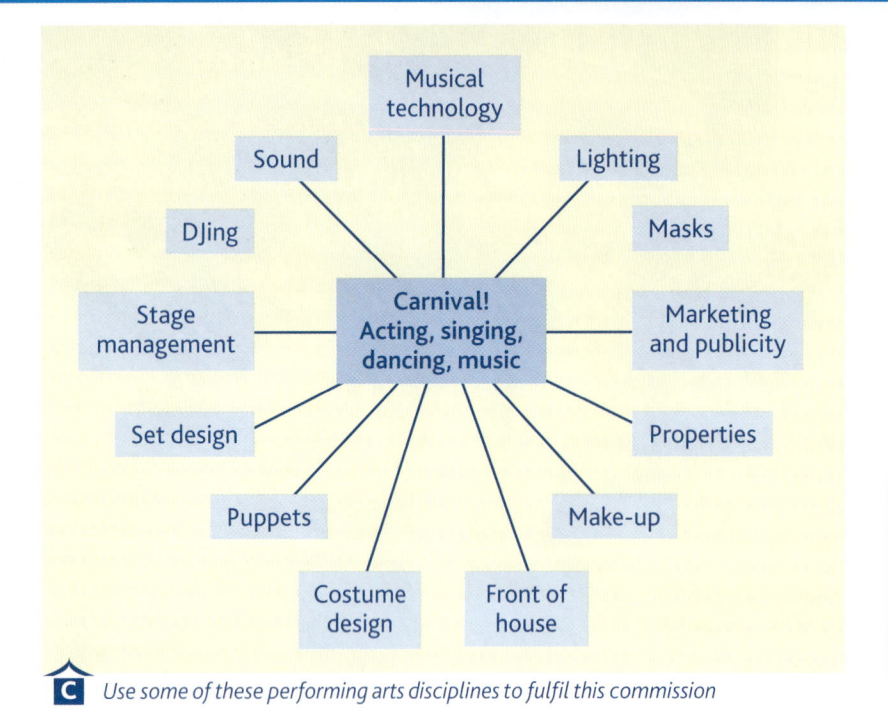

Spider diagram with centre "Carnival! Acting, singing, dancing, music" connected to: Musical technology, Sound, Lighting, DJing, Masks, Stage management, Marketing and publicity, Set design, Properties, Puppets, Make-up, Costume design, Front of house.

C Use some of these performing arts disciplines to fulfil this commission

Remember
Even though all the disciplines are shown in the spider diagram, they don't all have to be used. Base the included skills around those your company has to offer.

Activity

1 Production meeting

Hold a production meeting to determine the skills the different members of your team have to offer towards this project as shown above. List all the group's skills.

Update your skills audit based on work completed for the other practice commissions. Refer back to page 53 and carry on adding information to your CV.

AQA Examiner's tip
Minute your production meetings and make sure that everybody has a copy for their portfolios. However, you cannot take credit for work that you have not done, so always acknowledge who has done what out of your team.

D Dancers in Rio de Janeiro, Brazil

Chapter 7 Carnival! 79

Step 1 Research

Now you need to research the theme more carefully. Remember the more detailed your research, the easier it will be for you to write your two proposals.

Activity

2 Research the theme

In small groups or as individuals, choose one of the following areas to research:

- What is a carnival?
- What types of performances are included?
- What styles of music are used?
- What is the purpose of a carnival?
- What countries are famous for carnival?
- How does a carnival reflect a specific country?
- Are there any similarities between different countries?
- Select one country and research in more detail about its culture – for example, religion, national costume, food and drink, way of life, music, rituals, beliefs.

Prepare a short PowerPoint presentation, 'Carnival', for your fellow company members and the commissioner based on your research.

Extension activity

1 Think about the different forms of celebration of culture that take place in your area. Does your town have a carnival? Is Chinese New Year celebrated? If you can, find out when this takes place, go along and watch. Take photographs and then annotate and write about your experiences for your portfolio. If you take the ideas and show how you have used them, you can gain marks for 'contextual understanding of work-related aspects'.

F *The Lord Mayor's Show*

Did you know

The word 'carnival' comes from an Italian phrase. Catholics started the tradition of holding a wild costume festival before the first day of Lent. As Catholics are not supposed to eat meat during Lent they called their festival *Carnevale* which means to 'put away the meat'. As these carnivals became famous, they spread all over the world and each country added their own traditions to the celebration.

E *Chinese New Year*

Extension activity

2 Working in small groups, list all the different styles of performance that make up a carnival. Then split the list between the groups and research each one. Use images to support your research.

links

Venice Carnival: http://www.carnivalofvenice.com

Luton Carnival: http://www.luton.gov.uk/carnival

Leeds Carnival: http://www.leedscarnival.co.uk

Rotterdam Carnival: http://www.zomercarnaval.nl/nl/index.php

Viareggio Carnival, Italy: http://www.viareggio.ilcarnevale.com/index.cfm

www.carnivalpower.com

Now you have researched the theme of the commission you need to research local performance spaces and ways that you can present your performance. Think about the theme. Carnival is associated with celebration and street processions. Is there a space where you can perform outside?

Activity

3 Research performance spaces

As a production team, list the different performance spaces that are available in your area. Each member of the team must go away and discover more information about each space e.g. local parks, fields, streets.

Things to think about:

- What is the name and address of the space?
- Where is the space?
- What type of space is it (for example, a school hall, village hall or field)?
- Is it easily accessible for all the community?
- What does it cost to hire it?
- What are the health-and-safety regulations?
- What is the size of your performance space and what kind of facilities are there (for example, toilets or changing rooms)?
- Is any equipment included, for example lighting?

When you have all done this, feed back to each other in a group and choose the venue to use. Make sure that you say why you have chosen the venue.

Put all the information into your portfolio but make sure that you add a paragraph explaining that you divided the research between your production company members.

AQA Examiner's tip

Take photos of each venue from different perspectives – audience and performer – to put in your portfolio. Make sure that you annotate them!

Refer back to page 36 for ideas of different ways to perform. Keep referring back to the commission making sure you meet the requirements and the target audience.

You now need to think about how you can present your performances. Carnivals are usually long processions. Could you present your work in a different format that involves your audience? What about a **promenade performance**?

Key terms

Promenade performance: the performance takes place in different areas and the audience walk around to watch each section.

Activity

4 Research promenade performances

Research what a promenade performance is and write a list of the advantages and disadvantages of performing in this way. Give an example of how you could present a promenade performance to fit in with the commission and present your ideas to your production company.

G Notting Hill Carnival, London

Activity

5 Research target audience

Your target audience is the local community. This could be anything from toddlers to senior citizens so the content has got to appeal to all.

Look at the different performances that are available in your area. Gather flyers and posters from your local theatres or cuttings from the newspapers and look at the type and style of events on offer.

When you have done this, sort them into different age categories and look at the way each one is advertised: colours, type setting, pictures, famous names. You can copy these ideas and use them for your portfolio to help you gain some marks for the 'contextual understanding of work-related aspects'.

Activity

6 Involve the audience

If you are thinking about a promenade performance, then why not consider using the audience as part of your performance? Consider running a workshop with your audience before your performance. Include:

- mask/head-dress making
- information about carnivals
- your actors could introduce and inform the audience
- the dancers could teach some simple dance moves
- the singers could teach the chorus to a song.

Then let the audience join in with the procession at the end of your performance. You won't be able to rehearse this, so you must make sure that you think about all possible outcomes.

H *Mardi Gras floats, New Orleans*

Step 2 Planning and preparation

It is now time to gather all your research together and plan the two proposals you are going to present to the commissioner. Remember to constantly remind yourself of the commission and its requirements. Refer to page 58 for the detail that needs to be included in each of the proposals.

You will need to reflect on the proposal that the commissioner has chosen. Make sure that your portfolio includes both proposals and the information that the commissioner gave you as to why the proposal was chosen. It is very important that you respond to the commissioner's feedback about the reasons why one was chosen in preference to the other. You can then write your opinions to add more detail.

AQA Examiner's tip
When presenting your proposals to the commissioner, make sure that everyone is included in the presentation and that you present it in a professional manner.

Activity

7 Write about the proposal

When writing your opinions about the chosen proposal you could include the following:
- Why was the proposal chosen?
- Do you agree or disagree with the commissioner?
- If you agree with the commissioner's choice then say why. If you disagree with the commissioner's choice then say why and also why you think the other proposal should have been chosen.

Remember
You will need to hold regular meetings with your production company to review your progress constantly.

Activity

8 Devise costumes

Look at the costumes used in carnivals. They are usually 'larger than life' and full of colour. They have to be flexible so that the performer can move easily. Research the following for your portfolio:
- What materials are used for carnival costumes?
- How do the costumes work? When they are bigger than the person wearing the costume, how does the performer move in the costume?
- Do carnival costumes differ from country to country?

When you have looked into costumes, have a go at designing one – make sure that you colour and label it and describe how it moves.

If you can, find some material, feathers, foam and make your own costume or head dress. Remember to photograph every step of the process so you can put it into your portfolio.

Carnival costumes can make a big impact

Step 3 Rehearsal

The commissioner will have given you a set amount of time for the rehearsal period so a rehearsal schedule will need to be put into place. Remember to allow time for technical and dress rehearsals. It is also a good idea to rehearse in front of other people who can give you feedback.

Refer to Unit 2 to remind you of good rehearsal practice.

Activity

9 Record your rehearsals

With your stage manager, devise a rehearsal schedule for the number of rehearsals you have been allocated.

For each rehearsal, keep a diary log of your practice. Include the following information:

- the date
- the aims of the rehearsal
- any skills you developed
- professional practice, for example health and safety, warm up and warm down, rehearsing ideas from professionals
- what you actually achieved
- next steps.

> **Hint**
>
> Don't waste time! Make sure, at the beginning of the rehearsal period that everybody has something to do. Begin every rehearsal with a meeting and set yourself objectives for that the rehearsal. What do you want to achieve? It is important that you review your progress throughout and this can be used as evidence in your portfolio.

> **AQA Examiner's tip**
>
> If you write diary logs, make sure they are informative. If they are written properly you can gain marks for all assessment areas. You need to write about why you did something rather than just describing what you did.

Step 4 Shaping and polishing the performance

It is now time to run the performance. The more you get to run the show, the slicker it will be come. Bear in mind that if you are involving the audience, for example in a promenade performance, you will have to allow time for them to be settled before the next scene.

> **Remember**
>
> Refresh your memory of the process by looking back at the work that you did earlier in the course. You might find it useful to look at Unit 2.

Activity

10 Research a professional

Find a theatre using an internet search engine. Look for the list of personnel and find the name of the stage manager. Then either ring or email the person. Explain that you are studying performing arts and ask whether he/she would mind answering questions about their jobs and if they could send you a copy of a rehearsal schedule so that you can see how a professional one is laid out. You can then relate to the professional ideas as part of the 'contextual understanding of work-related aspects'.

Step 5 Dress and technical rehearsals

As mentioned before, make sure that your dress and technical rehearsals are organised in a professional way and that no time is wasted. This is really the time for the stage crew to mark up their set and practice the set changes and the lighting and sound crew to set their lights and microphones. Be prepared to go over things more than once and to rehearse the parts more important for them.

Activity

11 Collect audience feedback

Invite other classes to your dress rehearsal. If you are involving the audience in your performance then it is important to practice with an audience. Evaluate the rehearsal and get feedback from your audience. Make sure you include it in your portfolio!

AQA Examiner's tip

Remember that during the real moderation, your teacher and a moderator from the examination board will assess you using the assessment grid found in the specification. Your teacher has also acted as the commissioner and will know whether or not you have kept to the accepted proposal.

Step 6 The performance

It's performance time! Remember that the get in and get out are part of the performance and therefore part of your assessment. Refer back to chapter 5 on page 65 for the do's and don'ts. Remind yourself of the assessment strand for the performance and the accomplished way you have to present to the audience.

The Venice Carnival often uses different designs and has a different flavour to other carnivals. Consider what impression you want to make

Step 7 Evaluation

Look back to pages 66–67 to help you with your evaluation and the questions that need to be answered. Make sure that you evaluate your own contribution throughout the project and the contribution of others in your group. Don't forget to evaluate the skills you have learnt along the way!

Activity

12 Devise audience questionnaire

Devise a questionnaire about your performance to hand to your audience. You can add the feedback into your evaluations. You can also include the questionnaire as part of your planning and preparation.

K *The flag carriers at the Rio carnival represent their dance companies, and perform their own dances. Consider the roles in your performance*

UNIT FOUR

8 Final performance/designs for the

Objectives

In this section you will learn:

to prepare for the final showcase performance of the chosen commission

to prepare for moderation.

Remember

Your teacher is very important as a resource, to advise and answer questions. The teacher will be marking you for your skills development and professional conduct during the process.

As you start this unit you should remember that all the work that you are about to undertake builds on everything that you have done so far. The research and exploration of ideas that you carry out for this commission will be added to the work already completed for the practice commissions in your portfolio for Unit 3.

The starting point for this unit is to read the commission set by AQA carefully and remember to record everything that you plan and do in your portfolio. It is expected that you will show an awareness of how to:

- plan a response to the commission
- research venues
- research suitable materials including the work of others
- select and use suitable materials from different sources
- choose and develop ideas, using relevant techniques, or learn new methods where necessary to produce the final pieces
- present the final piece to the highest possible standard
- evaluate the response to the commission.

The rehearsal and preparation period should take approximately 30 hours and this should include any dress and technical rehearsals. Your final performance should take place in front of your target audience and at your chosen venue. If this is not available then you will probably perform in your school hall laid out as far as possible as if it were the chosen venue. As you work through this process you will find it useful to look at the assessment criteria for this unit and check them from time to time during the planning and preparation of your final performance or designs.

AQA Examiner's tip

All the work that you do in preparation for the final showcase performance should be included in your portfolio.

chosen commission

Planning and preparation

Starter activity

Read the notes from AQA

It is important that you read through all the notes provided in the paper set by AQA:

- highlight the important aspects of the commission notes
- list the roles and responsibilities that you will need to meet the requirements of the commission
- organise a production company meeting to discuss possible content of the performance.

Once you are happy that you understand the demands of the Commission notes you should follow the process that you worked with in Unit 3. If you follow the 'seven steps to success' you will be in a strong position to achieve the best possible results.

The next stage in the process is to prepare the **two** proposals to offer to your teacher who will act as the commissioner. Remember to work to the company's strengths and be clear about what you want to achieve. Your teacher will make the final decision as to the proposal that you will work on and once that decision has been made you will have to have very good reasons for changing your proposal.

The final performance must allow all the members of your company to demonstrate their strengths. Your teacher will be able to advise you about the choices that you should make and why.

Ask your teacher to discuss the details given in the specification to help you plan your final performance.

Solo and group presentations can be included as part of the commission. Group members should be aware of how all the pieces will fit into the final performance and the progress of others within the company.

When the commissioner has chosen one of the two proposals, you should be ready to enter the rehearsal period. Refer back to the practice commissions to remind yourself of the process. It is very important to keep your notes, research materials, designs, cue sheets, plans, minutes of meetings, observations and references to work-related issues as these will add to the evidence in your portfolio. This will also form the basis of your evaluation.

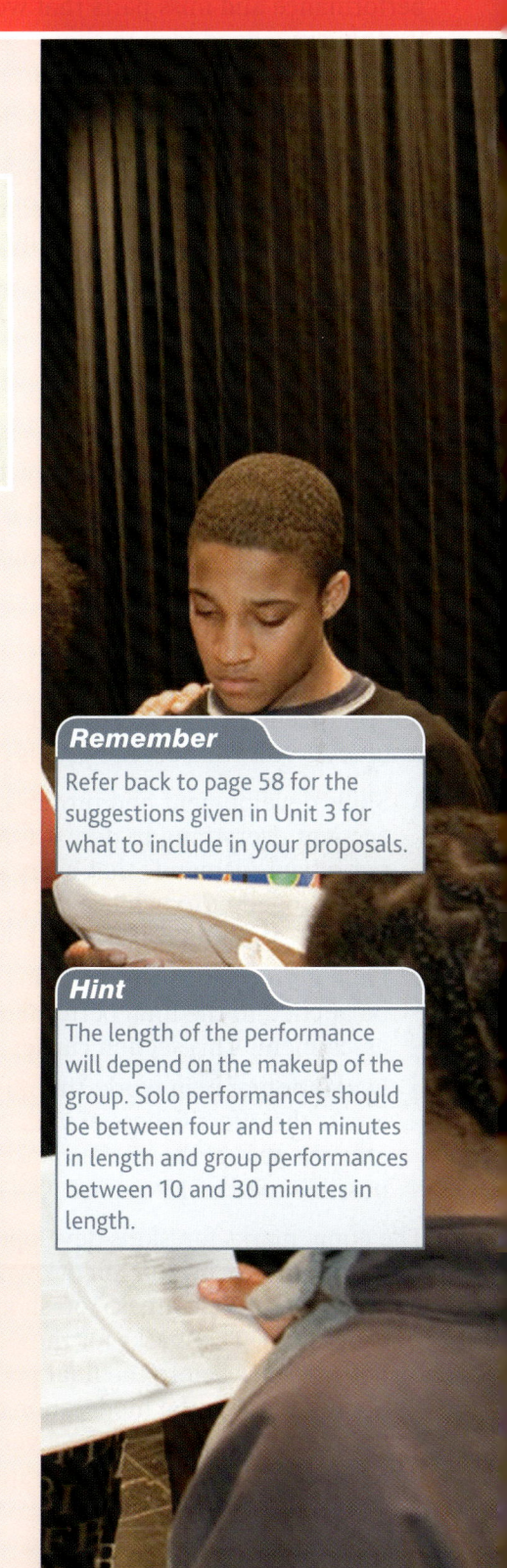

Remember

Refer back to page 58 for the suggestions given in Unit 3 for what to include in your proposals.

Hint

The length of the performance will depend on the makeup of the group. Solo performances should be between four and ten minutes in length and group performances between 10 and 30 minutes in length.

It is important to be aware of the time you are spending in rehearsal as sometimes you can over-rehearse some aspects of a performance and miss parts that would benefit from extra time. It is always a good idea to show your work to other members of the group and share your ideas. This will help you to focus your work. Your final performance should have energy and a freshness that engages your audience. The piece should be well rehearsed, the designs well prepared and everything should fit the original commission. Provided that you have continued to work through the process carefully and build on the skills that you have learned throughout the course you should achieve some very exciting moments in performance.

Assessment criteria

The final section of the brief is a copy of the assessment criteria and your teacher will explain how this works. You will be allocated marks for the following three areas:

- skills development and professional conduct
- final performance/design
- evaluation of own work.

You need to look carefully at the assessment grid because it sets out very clearly what is expected and how to achieve the best results. As you will see, the grid is divided into three main areas:

- Skills development and professional conduct: this takes into account everything to do with the preparation and rehearsal period and demands that every member of your company works together to achieve the best possible results. This section carries a possible total of 15 marks.
- Final performance/designs: this sets out the criteria that will be applied to the final performance and designs presented for assessment. This section carries a possible total of 30 marks.
- Evaluation of own work: this allows you to review and assess the effectiveness of your contribution to the overall effectiveness of the performance. This section carries a possible total of 15 marks.

The equal marks for 'skills development and professional conduct' and for 'evaluation of own work' emphasise the importance of these areas. You should give them appropriate consideration. The marks for these two areas will be decided by your teacher before the final performance and offered for moderation on the moderation day. The mark for 'final performance/ designs' will be given by your teacher and moderated by the visiting moderator appointed by AQA.

Chapter 8 Final performance/designs for the chosen commission 89

> **Activity**
>
> **1 Evaluate your contribution**
>
> All members of the company must prepare an evaluation of their contribution to planning, preparation and skills development. Your evaluation must be presented on one side of A2, two sides of A3 or four sides of A4. You will also need to provide three observations of your working practices during rehearsals by people with whom you have worked.

Moderation day

The process for the moderation day is exactly the same as you experienced when you performed your showcase performance. Provided that you have worked hard over the two years of the course you will be well prepared for this final performance. Make sure that everything is in place for a smooth-running show and that all your designs have been realised. You are about to complete a journey that, no doubt, had moments of uncertainty, which you have overcome in the final preparations for your performance.

A *Good luck for a great performance!*

Glossary

A

Allegory: the use of simple symbolic characters or stories to explain and illustrate a more complex idea.

Amphitheatre: an open-air building based on Greek and Roman architecture, with a central space for the presentation of dramatic or sporting activities.

Annotate: summarise, in your own words, notes that give further explanation of printed material.

Annotated: printed materials such as scripts, downloaded information and source materials that you have made notes on to assist your understanding when carrying out research during the course. An annotated text will be accepted as part of your portfolio work as it shows that you have considered the content of the text and have some understanding of it.

Arena: an area, surrounded on three sides by seating, in which a performance, entertainment or sporting event takes place (see also **amphitheatre**).

Audience participation: moments when the audience takes part in the action and contributes to the performance on stage.

B

Banksy: an artist famous for the high quality of his graffiti art. His work often reflects images from life, is highly regarded and is protected by local authorities against damage. Others imitate his work.

Beginners: the people required in the first scene.

Blocking: planning and rehearsal of the moves of the performers and recording them in the stage manager's book.

The Book: all the information needed to ensure that the performance goes smoothly; it is kept by the stage manager and is also referred to as the stage copy, the 'bible' or the prompt copy.

Book musical: a form very dependent on plot and character that integrates the script with the musical themes; popular in the mid-20th century.

Buskers: musicians who play under license in public places such as shopping centres and tube stations.

C

Choreography: a sequence of dance steps or movements created for performance.

Cirque du Soleil: a French-Canadian performing arts group famous for their exciting mix of traditional circus skills, mask work, storytelling and original music in performance.

Classical Greek theatre: a typical theatre of the 5th century BCE, such as the one in Epidaurus in Greece.

Commission: a special assignment that is given to a person or a group.

Commissioner: the person or group that asks you to take part in the performance event and sets the constraints for the performance.

Cue sheet: a list of actors' lines, musical effect, set or choreography and the technical task to be carried out when the line is spoken or an action completed.

D

Devised production: a performance piece that has been created by adapting and combining ideas and extracts from other sources through workshops and improvisation.

F

Focus: full concentration on the task in hand.

G

Genre: a style of theatre, such as a play, musical, opera, ballet, pop concert, comedy or pantomime.

Get-in: rigging or putting up the set and lights for a production.

Get-out: striking the set and rigging at the end of a production.

M

Musical theatre: an art form whose action and dialogue is interspersed with singing and dancing.

O

Observation: a short written report by a teacher or a member of your performing arts group commenting on your work.

P

Paralympics: an international athletic competition for athletes with disabilities.

Performance proposals: written documents that set out your ideas for the performance. Each proposal should include a brief description of the ideas to be included in the performance and any special technical requirements.

Personal skills audit: a personal 'checklist' of the skills that you are good at and those that will need to be improved as you work through the course.

Popular references: words, phrases or songs that a modern audience will recognise and identify with.

Portfolio: a record of the work that you have completed during the course.

Glossary

Practice brief: example of the kind of pieces set by the awarding body for practical assessment in Unit 2 and forming the basis of the portfolio evidence that you collect in Unit 1.

Practice commission: example of the kind of work that you will include in your portfolio for Unit 3 and that provide opportunities for you to prepare for the commission set for Unit 4.

Production company: the group that you will work with to develop the ideas that will be rehearsed and performed; it takes responsibility for all aspects of the production that you are about to undertake.

Production meetings: meetings where all the company members will discuss issues that arise, record their thoughts and plan the performance. Minutes of these meetings should be dated and kept safely in your portfolio.

Promenade performance: the performance takes place in different areas and the audience walk around to watch each section.

R

Roles and responsibilities: the jobs that you undertake as part of your production company.

Run: a rehearsal or performance that brings every aspect of the piece together; in the dress run, the performers work in their costumes; in a technical run, the technical team rehearses the lighting and sound cues and any special effects.

S

Screever: a licensed artist who draws with chalks on pavements and public areas. The pictures are usually of famous paintings, portraits of personalities or optical illusions. Screevers often draw onto canvas and carry their work away at the end of the day.

Short list: the list of ideas that the production company has decided to include in the final performance – the best ideas uncovered by the research.

Showcase: a performance that is created to show the skills of the group to best advantage; it has a theme and structure that suits the demands of the given brief.

Showcase performance: the programme of pieces that are rehearsed and shown in the final performance.

Skills audit: a detailed check or inspection of what skills you have as an individual and as a group.

Stage crew: the stage management and sound and lighting technicians.

Stock character: a stereotype that the audience expects to see.

T

Teching: the technical management of the whole show undertaken by the stage crew.

Theatre in education (TIE): a show developed around an educational topic or debate.

V

Venue: the location where the performance space can be found; it might be a theatre, a hall or a park.

W

Witness statement: a description of your progress and skills development that can be written by a teacher, parent or friend. Even the caretaker may wish to write about how well you have cleared away after rehearsals!

Index

A
advertising 81
agencies for children 40
Aladdin 33, 34
allegory 43
amphitheatre 18
annotate 31
annotated 18
arena 16
assessment criteria 48, 89
audience
   expectations 33
   feedback 84, 85
   identification 33, 40
   involvement 81
   participation 33
   target 81

B
Banksy 55
beginners 38
blocking 19, **34**, 35, 73
Boal, Augustus 39
book musical 71
Book, The 19, **22**, 23, 59
Brecht, Bertolt 39, 44
briefs 16, 31, 39, 47
buskers 55

C
careers website 72
Carnival 76
central character 43
chandelier 70
Chariots of Fire 19
Choreography 19
Cirque du Soleil 18
Classical Greek theatre 16
clearing up 28, 38, 52
commission 53, 58, 68, **69**, 76
   working to 50-67
commissioner 52, 71
contextual understanding 72
costumes, devising 82
courage 45
cue sheet 62
CV building 53

D
dancers' warm up 25
design skills 36
devised production 42, **43**
diary log 83
dress rehearsals 27, 38

E
evaluation 12, 29, 38, 45, 49, 66-7
   own work 29, 88
every child matters 39
Everyman 43

F
films 19, 57
final performance 46-7, 86-7
focus 38
front-of-house management 37, 60

G
genre 32
get-in 38, 52
get-out 38, 52
glossary 90-1

H
health and safety 60
house management team 37, 60

L
lighting 36

M
management skills 37
marketing 37
moderation day 49, 89
multiskilling 34
music, using 21, 44
Musical Theatre 68, **69**
My Fair Lady 72, 73

O
observation 24, **62**
Oldham Coliseum 33
Olympic Games 16

P
pace of a performance 20
pantomime 31-8
   conventions 35
   origins 32
Paralympics 18
performance 28, 38, 65, 75
   final 46-7, 86-7
   proposals 52, 77
   review 73
   skills 36
performing arts disciplines 8, 54, 78
personal skills audit 9, **16**, **34**
photos, using 80
plays, ancient Greek 43
popular references 33
portfolio **8**, 14
   building 10-11
posters 33
practice brief 7
practice commission 7
presentations 19, 58, 71
production company 16
production meetings 19, 20, 22, 54
production skills 37
promenade performance 80
prompt copy 19, **22**, 23, 59
proposals 82
   presenting 58, 71
publicity 37

R
record keeping 74
recording progress 24, 48
rehearsals 35, 59, 83
   dress 27, 38
   technical 27, 37
research 18, 55, 70, 79, 80
risk assessment 60
roles and responsibilities 12, **22**, 65
run **22**, 26, 63
running order 59
running time 21

S

screever 55
script 35, 59
seven steps to success 15, 51
shaping and polishing 26, 36, 42, 63, 75
short list 20
showcase 8
showcase performance 14, 16
skills audit 9, 16, 34
   reviewing 67
skills development 48
Sondheim, Stephen 72
songs 44
sound 37
spider diagrams 54, 78
stage copy 19, **22**, 23, 59
stage crew 41
stage management 37
stage manager 22, 37, 83
stock character 34
storytelling devices 43
street artists 56
Street life 52

T

teching 41
technical rehearsal 27, 37
technical skills 36-7
teenage problems 44
Theatr Clwyd 33
theatre companies 40
theatre in education (TIE) 39, 40, 42
time constraints 59
timing 87, 88

V

venue 16, 80

W

warm up 24, 25, 75
websites 72, 75, 79
West Side Story 57
witness statement 24
workshops 81